Occasionally, a writer comes along with such a keen insight into the Christian life you marvel at its impact on your life as you read each page. God has highly gifted Jan to write such a one that reveals the closeness of His presence in our joys, sorrows, and even the mundane. She beautifully writes with Biblical clarity and vulnerable candor based on her years of ups and downs.
Get this book if you want to understand and experience what it means that God is "with you" every moment. You will love it so much that you will want to pass it on to everyone you know!

Mark Maulding

Bestselling author, *God's Best-Kept Secret: Christianity is Easier Than You Think*

President of Grace Life International

I'm so excited about Jan's latest work, <u>Glory in Disguise</u>. You'll be inspired by the refreshing passages of Scripture and encouraged by the wisdom of the stories. But even more, you're going to be delighted - not just by the writing and personality Jan reveals, but by the astounding grace - God's glory in disguise - unveiled on each page. And in that dance with God through each encouraging nugget you'll find yourself as I did, one step further into the joy of a divine embrace of grace with Christ.

Mike Q. Daniel

Ministry consultant, event speaker, pastoral coach, & discipleship equipper

Mike Q. Daniel Ministries & The MQD Group

I am so happy to endorse the writings of Jan Loyd as she has been my dearest gift from God along with Penny Mandeville, who has written the sweet poetry for Jan's new book. I could not feel more fortunate to have the blessings of their messages for many years. Jan and Penny truly personify the goodness of God in the way they live their lives, their knowledge of scripture and their dedication to

their love of Jesus. I look forward always to Jan's writings and am sure you will too....as they always are so comforting and inspirational.
Pamela Bailey Kish
Staff Director, Office of The Dean of the House, Chairman Don Young of Alaska
U.S. Congress, retired

The messages of "Glory in Disguise" by Jan Loyd and Penny Mandeville speak deeply to the soul, giving living water to the thirsty. The author-poet friends tell stories based on their lives and develop them into encouragements for us all to rest in God's love and freedom in Christ.
The friends keep pointing to the grace of God and God-given discernment while also encouraging the reader to reflect on what characterizes those living as God's beloved.
Time and again I found myself wanting to share these stories and poems with those close to my heart ...
Eeva Duddleston
Mentor, retired educator, and cross cultural witness

Jan writes from her heart and her life. EVERY devotion is a testimony of how Our Lord works in her day-by-day experiences, and therefore, carries a promise that He can and will work in my life. It is the only devotional book that has ever affected me in this way. It was as if Jan was simply sharing walking and talking with Jesus. What a privilege...she somehow invites each one of us to walk with them.
Donna M. Heinz
Farmer's wife, retired teacher

This is not your run-of-the mill devotional! By weaving together her own simple personal experiences, solid biblical teaching, and application, Jan has designed an interactive devotional that helps the reader discover spiritual gems of truth, wisdom, and grace from the "ordinariness" of life. Her easy- to- do "exercises" in several of the entries-- listen to a YouTube song, watch a sunset, speak a blessing to someone, or "wash another's feet" (no water required), to name a few -- really bring to life the very essence of that day's theme. Not to mention the inspired poems written by Penny which complete each day's entry with beauty. Together these two dear ladies have created something that connects the reader to the loving heart of our Heavenly Father, and it is wonderful.

Robin Brown
Retired language arts teacher

I was moved deep in my soul by the insight and spiritual depth gleaned from everyday occurrences. Each meditation was profoundly edifying.

Pam Pillette
Missionary wife

In <u>Glory in Disguise</u>, Jan and Penny have collaborated on a beautifully uplifting book of devotions and poetry. Their words are an encouragement and guide to those seeking trust in the One who brings total rest and solace in chaos; joy and peace during duress; and salvation through His Son, Jesus Christ. Readers are certain to find comfort from the writers' testimonies, poems, and truths rooted in God's Word.

Blondezena Williams
Administrative Assistant, *Lighthouse* Community Church

Jan is a trusted spiritual guide. Her writings are born out of real-life circumstances and happenings, deep truths from scripture, and an

intimate relationship with the living Christ. She draws from sources as diverse as early church fathers to present day pop singers, and weaves them together into a beautiful tapestry of truth that will challenge, encourage, and deepen your experience of living in union with Christ. I whole-heartedly recommend this devotional!
Kathe Bricker
Precept Upon Precept Bible study leader

If you are a Christian woman and suffer from stress and anxiety issues, this book will be of excellent help to overcome those times of nervous tension... Jan and Penny point to real life experiences which many women face as well...Throughout the book, Jan and Penny point to God's Glory working in your life in the midst of each day to ward off the undesirable thinking.
Ron Hoffman
Retired Regional Director
American Missionary Fellowship/Infaith Mission

Jan Loyd's book <u>Glory in Disguise</u> is a collection of sixty meditations on the quiet, wonderful work of our loving Father. Jan's stories and insights, the accompanying poetry by her friend Penny Mandeville, and the exercises and reflections at the end of each meditation will challenge, stir, and comfort the heart of the reader. Jan's faith is not frothy and superficial but hard-won and genuine. <u>Glory in Disguise</u> is the book for someone seeking a deeper relationship with the God who can be trusted.
Paul Pyle
Pastor of Discipleship
Patterson Park Church, Dayton, OH

I love [Jan's] transparency and ability to see God's message in the day-to-day experiences of life. <u>Glory in Disguise</u> reveals the extraordinary by viewing the ordinary at times through a spiritual

microscope and at other moments through a divine telescope in order to gain God's perspective on reality. Jan has captured God's glory in her family; in her dream to be a dancer; in salt, light, stars, and the beach; in cancer; in sunrises and sunsets; in the art of teaching; and in the relationships we see all around us every day. ... Each chapter concludes with action steps including projects, journaling prompts, and additional book suggestions. I believe that this devotional book could be utilized as a year-long map for spiritual growth ...The time spent will yield precious jewels that will be both challenging and inspiring to your heart.
David Rough, Ed.D.
Academic Dean, Retired, Dayton Christian Schools

Glory in Disguise

Seeing God in Our Every Day

By

Jan Loyd and Penny Mandeville

Published by *A Branch in the Vine*, 2023

Glory in Disguise
Second edition, January 11, 2025

Author Jan Loyd
Poet Penny Mandeville
Cover designer Jeremy Loyd www.jeremy@jloyd.net

Jan

To my precious children Jeremy J. Loyd and Elizabeth Loyd Filson.
Thank you for teaching me what the love of God is all about.
I love you more than life.

Penny

To my husband, Geoff.
Your stability, strength, wisdom and support have been the
encouragement
and grounding I have always needed.
After 53 years of marriage,
I have come to recognize this more and more every day.
I thank the Lord for you.

Scripture Quotations

Scripture quotations taken from the Amplified® Bible (AMP), Copyright © 2015 by The Lockman Foundation. Used by permission. lockman.org

Scripture quotations marked CSB have been taken from the Christian Standard Bible®, Copyright © 2017 by Holman Bible Publishers. Used by permission. Christian Standard Bible® and CSB® are federally registered trademarks of Holman Bible Publishers.

Scripture quotations are from the ESV® Bible (The Holy Bible, English Standard Version®), copyright © 2001 by Crossway, a publishing ministry of Good News Publishers. Used by permission. All rights reserved.

Scripture quotations taken from the (NASB®) New American Standard Bible®, Copyright © 1960, 1971, 1977,1995, 2020 by The Lockman Foundation. Used by permission. All rights reserved. lockman.org

Scripture quotations marked (NLT) are taken from the *Holy Bible*, New Living Translation, copyright ©1996, 2004, 2015 by Tyndale House Foundation. Used by permission of Tyndale House Publishers, Carol Stream, Illinois 60188. All rights reserved.

Scripture quotations marked MSG are taken from *The Message*, copyright © 1993, 2002, 2018 by Eugene H. Peterson. Used by permission of NavPress. All rights reserved. Represented by Tyndale House Publishers

Table of Contents

*When we walk in the Lord's presence,
everything we see, hear, touch, or taste
reminds us of Him.
This is…a life in which nothing, absolutely nothing,
is done, said, or understood independently of Him
who is the origin and purpose of our existence.*[2]
Henri Nouwen,
The Living Reminder

A Letter to our Readers

Dear Reader

Welcome to *Glory in Disguise.* Thank you for joining us on this adventure of *Seeing God in Our Every Day.*

As you read, you will encounter real-life stories and illustrations, metaphors and poetry, and most importantly Scriptures. Each points to God Who is "manifest and notoriously active in our daily life."[1]

You may go at your own pace through this little volume and even vary the order of the meditations. The most important thing is to encounter the Lord today–maybe in surprising, unexpected, and hidden ways.

With prayers for open eyes and hearts,

Jan and Penny

GLORY IN OUR ORDINARY

*We encounter God in the ordinariness of life:
not in the search for spiritual highs and
extraordinary, mystical experiences, but in
our simple presence in life.*[3]
Brennan Manning,
Abba's Child

1. No Ordinary Rock: Shining in Your Every Day

God wanted to make known…the glorious wealth of this mystery,
which is Christ in you, the hope of glory.
Colossians 1:27 CSB

Our daughter Beth became a rock collector sometime in her childhood. I'm not sure what drew her to rocks of every kind. Maybe those family car trips to Arizona to visit grandparents over the years? Her heavy box labeled "ROCKS" testifies to all the years and places that added to her unique collection.

I have to admit, to me a rock has always been just a rock. But I discovered otherwise through Beth's rocks. I learned that rocks aren't always what they seem to be. One of her rocks was an "Obsidian." Held up to the light, a person could see right through it.

My favorite of all Beth's rocks was a seemingly ordinary rock called a "geode" –plain gray or brown with no distinguishing features to alert the untrained eye. Who knew this ordinary rock could be something special? And a geode is special. When a geode is cracked open, it reveals why –glory bursts forth. A shining treasure of crystals remains hidden in that ordinary rock until cracked open by a blow. Without the trauma, the rock will just stay unattractive, obscure, and unrevealed.

To me, a geode is a perfect picture of my ordinary, often unattractive, human life. In reality though, our glorious, extraordinary God dwells deep within. And as I walk with the Lord through the hard things in life, oh my! His glory peeks through. And at times, His glory bursts through, manifesting His life in surprising ways.

The Scriptures are replete with references to God's glory united with our humanness. We see it supremely in Jesus God's Son, our Lord and Savior. And because of Him and His indwelling life, God's glory now resides in His children by grace through faith. We are each unique "geode-ones." We contain our glorious God, who is continually revealed as we walk with Him through the trials of life.

My favorite passage of Scripture that speaks to this metaphor is 2 Corinthians, chapter 4.

> For God, who said, "Let light shine out of darkness," has shone in our hearts to give the light of the knowledge of the glory of God in the face of Jesus Christ.
>
> But we have this treasure in jars of clay [*geode rocks*], to show that the surpassing power belongs to God and not to us.
>
> We are afflicted in every way, but not crushed;
> perplexed, but not driven to despair;
> persecuted, but not forsaken;
> struck down, but not destroyed;
> always carrying in the body the death of Jesus, so that the life of Jesus may also be manifested in our bodies.
>
> For we who live are always being given over to death for Jesus' sake, so that the life of Jesus also may be manifested in our mortal flesh.
> So death is at work in us, but life in you…
> 2 Corinthians 4:6-12 NASB (emphasis added)

Our geode-like humanness gets banged up, cracked, broken open, and even "pulverized" at times. But through it all, God is being revealed as the powerful One as we cling to Him. Even when we don't see it, others do. And that's the point, isn't it? The hidden Lord lives in us by faith. He empowers us and shows forth the glorious reality of Who He is through our human, banged up, "geode-like" life.

What about you, my friend? Do you feel the breaking going on in your life? Don't despair. Trust your glorious God to "shine through your cracks." He is with you and shines through you in whatever you face today.

<u>Hidden Beauty</u>
The mystery in me
Only He can see
And only He has known.

The beauty He sees
Is surely not me
But is He who calls me His own.
  Penny Mandeville

<u>Prayer</u>
O Lord God, Creator of my ordinary geode-like soul. Thank You that Your glory is hidden in me, just waiting to be revealed. What a privilege to be the container and expresser of Your Life on this earth. Remind me of Your Powerful Presence now and always. I chose to trust You today for whatever may come my way. In Jesus' shining Name. Amen.

<u>Reflections</u>
1. Ask the Lord to reveal to you how He is showing forth His glory through your humanness. Think of your talents, your personality,

your circumstances, your relationships. Yes, even your weakness and your trials.

2. Yield to Him the people and circumstances in your life that are causing you stress.

3. Thank Him for the privilege of being the container and expresser of His Life on this earth.

2. Children Incognito: Living an Adult Life

Jesus said, "Let the children come to me. Don't stop them!
For the Kingdom of Heaven belongs
to those who are like these children."
Matthew 19:16 NLT

One day, my husband John came home from work and said, "I'm going to Shanghai next week for work."

"Where?" I was shocked.

"Shanghai." he repeated.

Neither John nor I have ever been world travelers. So the idea of his going alone to Shanghai was terrifying to both of us.

As he was preparing to go, our small fellowship group prayed over him. They encouraged John to trust the Lord in this test of faith.

I took John to the Dayton airport very early the morning of his departure. After he checked his bags, I cried, kissed him good-by, and prayed. John slowly made his way in the serpentine line to get scanned. Then he would be out of sight and on to the gate.

There he was -- my tall, kind, gentle soul of a husband. I knew he was scared, and I was scared for him. All of a sudden, as clear as a bell, the still small *Voice* of the Spirit entered my consciousness:

> John is just a little child, locked up in an adult body,
> trying to live an adult life in an adult world.

What did that mean? I would soon find out.

When I walked out of the airport to the car, the early morning pitch-blackness had been transformed into the most beautiful, crystal-clear spring morning. I just couldn't go back home on the interstate on a morning like this. So I went north on country roads, not quite knowing where I'd end up.

I soon found myself in the parking lot of one of my favorite places: Charleston Falls Nature Preserve. Normally, I don't go to remote places by myself, but I sensed the *Voice* beckoning me on.

As I walked down the path, I thought of our newlywed daughter saying goodbye to her husband in his Air Force camouflage. Nate had been deployed overseas just a few days earlier. I felt Beth's distress as she said good-bye for what would be several months.

Again, the *Voice,*

> Beth and Nate are both little children, locked up in adult bodies, trying to live adult lives in an adult world.

I walked on. I thought of our young adult son just a few years earlier, diagnosed with thyroid cancer at age 20. He had been scared but trusting God.

> Jeremy is just a little child, locked up in an adult body, trying to live an adult life in an adult world.

With each new memory, the *Voice*…until the truth began to dawn upon me,

We are ALL little children, locked up in adult bodies, trying
to live adult lives in an adult world. And the only way we
can do that is to live as little children with our Abba Father
God.

Then I remembered Jesus, the Perfect Child of His Father. He lived
as a Child in an adult world. And the *Voice* revealed how.

Jesus lived secure in His Father's love.
For the Father loves the Son, and shows Him all things that
He Himself is doing.
 John 5:20 NASB

Jesus lived in total dependence upon His Father.
Jesus said, "The Son can do nothing by Himself; He can only
do what He sees His Father doing." John 5:19 NASB

Jesus lived with His Father in trust & vulnerability.
In the days of His flesh, He offered up both prayers and
supplications with loud crying and tears to the One who is
able to save Him from death, and He was heard because of
His reverence. Although He was a Son, He learned
obedience from the things He suffered. Hebrews 5:7 NASB

This is good news for those of us who are God's children. Jesus our
Savior, who is the Perfect Child of the Father, lives in you and me
by His Spirit. He lives His Child-life through us as we depend on
Him. We don't have to have it all together. We can be vulnerable
with our Father God. We can trust Him to enable us, through the
indwelling Spirit of His Son, to live an adult life in an adult world.

So beloved siblings in the family of God, fellow "children
incognito," do you ever feel scared and needy and helpless? Know

you are loved and cared for by your Father every day of your life. Trust Him. He cares for you.

> You are from God, little children, and…greater is He who is in you than he who is in the world. 1 John 4:4 NASB

<u>Dependent on God</u>
As a child I felt secure
Safe in my mother's arms.
No worries about the future
No reason to be alarmed.

Trusting both my parents
To take good care of me.
They were strong and wise enough
To handle what would be.

Now I'm grown and realize
Human wisdom's not enough.
I'm still dependent and need support
When things in life get tough.

But the Holy Spirit is in me
Reminding me He's there.
And Jesus is right beside me
Whenever I despair.

The Father bends a listening ear
To hear my every prayer.
They surround me and astound me
With their gentle loving care.
       Penny Mandeville

<u>Prayer</u>
Dear Father God, thank You for welcoming me into Your family. Thank You that I can live as a "child incognito," needy, yet dependent on You in this adult-sized world. It is so beyond me, and often scares me to death. But I chose to trust You today to live in and through me by Your Spirit. In Jesus, Your Son's Name. Amen.

<u>Reflections</u>
1. Journal the times this week when you have felt helpless, scared, anxious, alone. Come needy and dependent to your loving Father God, as a "child incognito."

2. Journal your prayers and then listen for His *Voice* who calls you, His beloved child.

GLORY IN NATURE

There is ecstasy in paying attention …
to see the world sacramentally,
to see everything as an outward and visible sign
of inward, invisible grace.[4]
Anne Lamott,
Bird by Bird

3. The Masterpiece: Rejecting Self-Rejection

For we are God's masterpiece.
He has created us anew in Christ Jesus,
so we can do the good things he planned for us long ago.
Ephesians 2:10 NLT

God is the sovereign Creator of all things. And our sovereign, Creator God loves His creation. And who can blame Him? His glorious creation displays His creativity, His sense of humor, His joy, His fun.

Can you just see the twinkle in His eye as He put each in its place? No wonder He said, "It is good." Not once but six times (Genesis 1:1-25):

1. God created light . . . "Good" (vs 4) – Recall the sudden appearance of a rainbow after the rain.
2. God created land and sea . . . "Good" (v 10) – Be amazed by the mountains rising up from the plain.
3. God created plants . . . "Good" (v 12) – Enjoy the fragrance of roses and the lusciousness of strawberries in season.
4. God created the sun, moon, and stars . . . "Good" (v 18) – Glory in sunrise over the ocean and brilliant stars on a black velvet sky.
5. God created birds and fish . . . "Good" (v 21) -- Smile at the haughty display of the proud peacock and the playful dolphins breaking the surface of the sea.
6. God created land animals . . . "Good" (v 25) Be amazed at God's endless variety, including pets galore.

But He wasn't finished, as delighted as He was with all He had made. He knew something was lacking -- His masterpiece, the epitome of His creation — man and woman. Together they manifest *the Imago Dei,* the image of God.

> So God created man in His own image, in the image of God He created him; male and female He created them.   Genesis 1: 27 NASB

And did you notice God's reaction when He completed His creation with the crafting of His image bearer?

> And God saw all that He had made, and behold, it was very good.
> Genesis 1:31 NASB

Not just good … very good. But I fear we humans, who are God's image bearers, are more characterized by self-rejection than self-acceptance. Why is that I wonder?

We don't like something about ourselves. Maybe it's our personality, our gender, our physical stature, our abilities. Maybe it's where we live, our family of origin, our profession, our income, even our "spirituality" or lack thereof. And we assume these are what give us our value, our identity.

But they are based on lies we believe because of how others have treated us. Or maybe our culture, our friends, our school, our leaders, and even family members and church leaders have fed us lies about our true identity.

One of my favorite devotional writers speaks to these very issues and causes us to look self-rejection square in the face:

> When we have come to believe in the voices that call us worthless and unlovable, then success, popularity, and power are easily perceived as attractive solutions. The real trap, however, is self-rejection. As soon as someone accuses me or criticizes me, as soon as I am rejected, left alone, or abandoned, I find myself thinking, "Well, that proves once again that I am a nobody." ... Self-rejection is the greatest enemy of the spiritual life because it contradicts the sacred voice that calls us the "Beloved." Being the Beloved constitutes the core truth of our existence.[5]
> Henri Nouwen, *Life of the Beloved*

This is a real eye-opener, isn't it? And in a very real sense, our self-rejection is rejection of our loving Creator God. He calls us His masterpiece, His beloved image bearer, hidden in our humanity.

> For we are God's masterpiece ["poema" in Greek]. He has created us anew in Christ Jesus, so we can do the good things he planned for us long ago. Ephesians 2:10 NLT

So dear friend, what lie is it you are believing, causing you to live in self-rejection rather than embracing God's love and delight in you? Reject the lie and live wholeheartedly from who you really are, your Creator's beloved masterpiece, the "poem" He is speaking in His beautiful world.

> See how very much our Father loves us, for he calls us his children, and that is what we are. 1 John 3:1 NLT

<u>My Beloved</u>
I am my Beloved's and my Beloved is mine.
The relationship sought since the beginning of time.

He offers it freely, His love and forgiveness
Others should accept it, but for me, I have missed it.

My sins are too many, too large and too bad.
Forgiveness for me is just not to be had.

So, you're saying My sacrifice wasn't enough?
Perhaps I should have died twice on that cross.

Oh, Jesus, My Savior. I was thinking all wrong!
Of course it's enough and to You I belong.

With assurance I say without looking behind
I am My Beloved's and My Beloved is mine.
       Penny Mandeville

<u>Prayer</u>
Lord, I embrace Your design for me, Your image bearer, Your masterpiece. Dispel the lies I have been believing and teach me to walk in Your truth and Your love every day. I receive Your words calling me Your Beloved. In Jesus' Name. Amen.

<u>Reflections</u>
1. Ask the Lord to reveal to you what it might be that you are rejecting about yourself – your personality, your appearance, your gender, your family, your present job, where you live, your abilities or lack thereof, etc.

Could this rejection be a result of comparing yourself to others?

2. Write these things down in your journal. Then go through one by one. Confess your self-rejection to the Lord, thanking Him for His forgiveness.

3. Then thank God for each and ask the Lord how He might be using them in your life. Record any insights He reveals.

4. The Reservoir: Recognizing Your Source

Anyone who is thirsty may come to me!
Anyone who believes in me may come and drink!
For the Scriptures declare,
'Rivers of living water will flow from his heart.'
John 7:37-38 NLT

My husband grew up in Globe, Arizona, a little mining town east of Phoenix. One of Globe's "claims to fame" is the amazing Roosevelt Dam, 30 miles northwest from the town. The Roosevelt Dam is on the Salt River and forms a reservoir, called Roosevelt Lake. The reservoir holds water for recreation, irrigation, power, etc.

John and I got into a discussion one night about the source of the water. I kept pressing him for an answer to my burning question:

"What is the source of the water that flows into the Roosevelt Dam and reservoir?"

His first answer was "the Salt River."

Then I asked what is the source of the Salt River?

He answered, "It is the confluence of the Black River and the White River."

And then, where is the source of those two rivers?

His answer, "Mountain streams from the White Mountains."

Then, where is the source of the mountain streams?

"Rain and snow and springs up on those mountains."

Aha! "Mother Nature." GOD. End of "discussion."

So I have been pondering,

> Who is my Source to do life? To be a friend? To do my job? To do marriage? To parent/grandparent? To live my life on this earth?

> Who is my Source for the rivers of life and love I crave?

My husband is not my source of life, and I am not his source. It's nice when we hit it right and make each other feel accepted and loved. But even that is short-lived if we are looking to each other to fill our love tank.

Only God is enough to fill my bottomless pit of need, and only God is enough to fill his bottomless pit of need. Really, no one on this earth is enough to fill my need for life and love — not my husband or kids or grandkids or relatives or friends or anyone. And I am not enough to fill anyone else's need for love — not my husband or kids or grandkids or relatives or friends or anyone.

If I expect someone to fill my bottomless pit of need, I can get grasping and needy and disappointed and bitter. And it can all go dark in my soul.

If I am trying to be someone else's bottomless source of life and love, I give out of obligation, not out of want to. I give to get approval or love. I try to keep the person ok so they don't get upset or disappointed. I rescue. And then it all gets heavy. I've been guilty of that and more.

But I've come to know a "healthy detachment." I no longer try to be "messiah" to loved ones and others. And it's because I have a "passionate attachment" to Christ who is my Source. "Christ in me" is the only One who can meet my deepest needs or the needs of those I love.

So then His promise is that out of my innermost being will flow rivers of Living Water…the Spirit. I can be God's instrument, the conduit of His Love to my loved ones and others. Then He is the Source. I am not and others are not.

> For in him the whole fullness of deity dwells bodily,
> and you have been filled in him, who is the head of all rule
> and authority.
> Colossians 2:9-10 ESV

So my friend, what about you? What/who are you looking to meet your deepest need for unconditional love, acceptance, worth/value, and security?

Look to the Lord Jesus Christ. And let others in your life "off the hook." Then you can receive everything that others and life offer you by the grace of God as free gifts.

And let yourself "off the hook," no matter what the others around you may expect from you. You were never meant to be their deepest need-meeter. Release them to God for that. But then ask the Lord what you can freely give to others out of love and from God's life in you and through you.

So expect all from God.

Receive all as free gifts from His hand.

And give freely from the life of the Loving God within you.

<u>He's the Only One</u>

God made us in His perfect design
To need Him desperately.
But we try to fill that need
With everything else we see.

We seek out love from others
Hoping it will bring
The satisfaction and fulfillment
That can only be done by Him.

He's the only one who loves us
In every way we can conceive.
The only one who can make us whole
If only we believe.

        Penny Mandeville

<u>Prayer:</u>

Lord God, I drink of You, my only True Source. You Alone are my Need-Meeter. I confess that I often look to significant people and things in my life to fill my emptiness. Thank you for Your forgiveness and Your Abiding Presence. By Your grace and indwelling Presence, use me as a conduit of your love and acceptance in the lives of others. In Jesus' full Name. Amen.

<u>Reflections</u>

1. Spend your week basking in the truth of your union with God though our Lord Jesus Christ.

2. Prayerfully relish each of the following truths and the Scriptures telling of the Lord's total provision for you, His child. HE is your Source. Journal how the Lord speaks to you.

Because I am in Christ…
I Am Loved
I am a child of God-John 1:12
I am beloved-Romans 9:25
I am chosen-Colossians 3:12
I am loved by God as much as Jesus is-John 17:23, 26
I am Jesus's friend-John 15:15
I am inseparable from God's love-Romans 8:37-39

I Am Acceptable
I am accepted by God-Romans 15:7
I am righteous-2 Corinthians 5:21
I am a saint-1 Corinthians 1:2; Ephesians 1:1 (NASB)
I am not condemned-Romans 8:1
I am completely forgiven-Colossians 2:13
I am holy and blameless-Ephesians 1:4

I Am Valuable
I am God's masterpiece-Ephesians 2:10 (NLT)
I am adopted-Ephesians 1:5
I am God's treasure-Matthew 13:44
I am God's pearl-Matthew 13:45-46
I am a new creation-2 Corinthians 5:17
I am designed by God-Psalm 139:13-16

I Am Secure
I am more than a conqueror-Romans 8:37
I am complete in Christ-Colossians 2:10
I am safe in Christ-Colossians 3:3-4
I am seated in the heavenly realms-Ephesians 2:6
I am eternally in Christ-John 10:28
I am united with Christ-1 Corinthians 6:17

Mark Maulding, *God's Best-Kept Secret*[6]

5. The Sunrise Club: Receiving Morning Mercies

> The faithful love of the Lord never ends!
> His mercies never cease.
> Great is his faithfulness;
> his mercies begin afresh each morning.
> Lamentations 3: 22-23 NLT

I have a Sunrise Club. My brother Conrad and I are charter members. Whenever I go to the coast in New Jersey, I must get up to see at least one sunrise. Often Conrad will call me to make sure I'm up, and he joins me. Through the years, various family members have joined the club. And each of them has fulfilled the basic requirement of seeing at least one sunrise.

You may ask why I love sunrises so much. To me a sunrise is a magnificent picture of the glory of our God, manifested in His beautiful creation.

> The heavens declare the glory of God,
> and the sky above proclaims his handiwork.
> [2] Day to day pours out speech,
> and night to night reveals knowledge.
> [3] There is no speech, nor are there words,
> whose voice is not heard.
> [4] Their voice goes out through all the earth,
> and their words to the end of the world.
> In them he has set a tent for the sun,
> [5]   which comes out like a bridegroom leaving his chamber,
> and, like a strong man, runs its course with joy.
> [6] Its rising is from the end of the heavens,
> and its circuit to the end of them,

and there is nothing hidden from its heat.
Psalm 19:1-6 ESV

Now there are beautiful sunrises everywhere. I've seen glorious sunrises with my grandson Kaden over the mountains to the east of their home in Menifee, CA. Recently, my husband John & I have viewed the early sunrise between mountain peaks in Tucson. And even here at home in Ohio, the colors of the rising sun can often amaze us with its glory.

However, as we East Coast sunrise watchers all know, the Cadillac of all sunrises takes place over the ocean. The vastness of the ocean and the littleness of me on the shore help to correct my perspective about God and my life. And the sunrise over the ocean speaks with new messages every day. I see and hear and feel and smell and even taste God there in a unique way.

In the moments leading into the actual breaking forth of the fiery sun-ball, there are constant changes in color, lighting, shapes, atmosphere. No two moments are the same, just as no two sunrises are the same. And then when the sun bursts forth out of the straight-line horizon of the ocean…wow! Glory indeed.

But many days we may be disappointed by no visible glory. The clouds, the rain, the fog, the haze may all obscure the rising of the sun. But we know the sun has still risen, often with a silvery beauty all its own.

How do we know that the sun has risen? By faith. Because we know the sun rises every day. And that's why I now love all sunrises. Each one is a picture of the glory of God and His fresh mercies. At times they are hidden, to be received by faith. But at other times they are manifested clearly, even dramatically.

Isn't that also true about life? Sometimes God manifests Himself in tangible ways, like in the love of a mother for her child, in an encouraging note from a friend, in a deep experience in prayer and worship. But then at other times, His glory is obscured, as in the death of a loved one, the suffering of rejection, the struggles of financial need. Then it is by faith we say, "I know that I know that...

> I know that my Redeemer lives, and that in the end he will stand upon the earth.
> Job 19:25 NIV

So here is my "take-away."

> God is unchangingly loving and merciful to me because that is who He is. But His mercies (His watch-care, His provision, His power, His presence, His intervention) do change "character." They are uniquely fitted for me and my specific need for my day.

> > His mercies are new every morning. Great is His faithfulness.
> > Lamentations 3:23 NASB

What is it that you need today, my friend? What does this day hold for you? Remember your merciful, loving, glorious, unchanging God is there for you with His unique provision for your day. He Himself is really all you need. He will meet you with fresh mercies for whatever you may face today. Trust Him.

Sunrise Promise

The sunrise holds a message for all of us to hear.
There's a promise in the new day
In the beauty that appears.

Even if the sky is dark with storm clouds, do not fear.
The sun still shines behind the clouds
And there the sky is clear.

Here's the promise of the Lord
For every new day of the year,
"Whatever circumstance you're weathering
God is always near."
        Penny Mandeville

Prayer

O Lord of the glorious rising sun, I receive You and Your glory and Your abundant mercies for this day. Even if the way is obscured, I'll trust You to take my hand and lead me through. I know You are with me even when You are not obvious. Lord, I believe. Help my unbelief.

In Your glory-filled Name. Amen.

Reflections

1. Set an alarm and get up early one morning and view a sunrise. Enjoy the glory of God in its amazing magnificence or the glory of God in its magnificent obscurity. Remember,

> ...faith is the assurance of things hoped for, the conviction of things not seen.
> Hebrews 11:1 ESV

2. Journal what you see and what the Lord says to you through the sunrise. Are there "fresh mercies" you can receive for your day? Thank Him. Ask Him for what you need.

3. And no matter what kind of sunrise it is, let me know if you'd like to join my Sunrise Club...or better yet, my SONrise Club. jan@abranchinthevine.com

6. Sunrise, Sunset: Remembering His Faithfulness

He who watches over you will not slumber…nor sleep.
The Lord is your protector;
The Lord is your shade on your right hand.
The sun will not beat down on you by day,
Nor the moon by night.
The Lord will protect you from all evil;
He will keep your soul.
The Lord will guard your going out and your coming in
From this time and forever.
Psalm 121:4-8 NASB

Sunrise, sunset,
Sunrise, sunset,
Swiftly flow the days ...

So goes the beautiful wedding song from the movie, *Fiddler on the Roof.* And so go our days, don't they? One day follows another – sunrise, sunset.

Sunrises have always been my thing. And every morning I am at a beach, the bonus is I get to experience sunrise after sunrise over the ocean. Each one is unique and special and "speaking."
But I do remember one evening at the beach, when I unexpectedly witnessed a glorious sunset over the bay.

The way it impacted me was a surprise. My usual focus was always on the fireball sun rising in the east, signaling the beginning of the new day with its corresponding "fresh mercies." But here I was, watching that same sun disappear into the western horizon of the bay. I was amazed!

So a new message in that same fiery ball. This time, the message was *gratitude* -- gratitude for the gift of the day that had unfolded, gratitude for the people I encountered, gratitude for the lessons I learned, gratitude for even the trials that tested me. All had been matched that day with fresh morning mercies by our faithful, unchanging God.

And so in those final moments of my day, I remembered God's love and acceptance and faithfulness. I had lived my day in His total forgiveness in Christ. I recalled His indwelling Presence as He carried my burdens moment by moment as I depended on Him.

And so, as has been my custom, I prayed Jesus' final prayer from the Cross, the prayer He most likely prayed as a child at His mother's knee.

"Father, Into Your hands I commit my spirit. Amen."

What about you, my friend? As you reflect on the closing of your day, do you remember God's abiding Presence with you? Do you recognize His fresh morning mercies that were equal to the situations that you faced? If so, thank Him. If not, ask Him to reveal Himself and how He was there all the time.

Counting Our Blessings
Each day tells a story
Of Christ's love and care for us.

From early morning sunrise
To the evening's quiet dusk.

Then all through the dark of night
Till the sun comes up again

He gives mercies every moment
From beginning to the end.

So as we go to bed at night
Before we fall asleep

Let's count the ways the Lord blessed us
Instead of counting sheep.
      Penny Mandeville

<u>Prayer</u>

Father God, Creator of oceans and bays, Creator of me. I commit my spirit into Your more than capable Hands. I rest in You, grateful for the day You have given me, the people who have graced my life, the circumstances that have been ordained by You for Your glory and my benefit. And I also thank You for all the "hard" – people and circumstances. Open my eyes to see You in my every day, even in the hard things. In Jesus' Almighty Name. Amen.

<u>Reflections</u>

1. View a sunset right where you are. Reflect on the events of the day. How did God meet you with His mercies, His presence? Thank Him.

2. Start making a list of mercies/blessings/gifts received each day. Then keep adding to it at the close of each day.

3. Find this song on Youtube, "Where Can I Go" (GLAD). Get your tissues ready. Journal your thoughts and prayers.

4. Maybe today brought darkness to your soul. Ask Him about it. Turn your focus to the Lord by faith. Thank Him for the small things. Commit to Him the hard things. Read Psalm 139: 11-12.

Sunrise, sunset, Sunrise, sunset
Swiftly flow the days
Seedlings turn overnight to sunflowers
Blossoming even as we gaze
Sunrise, sunset, Sunrise, sunset
Swiftly fly the years
One season following another
Laden with happiness and tears.[7]

"Sunrise, Sunset," *Fiddler on the Roof.*

7. The Rose: Letting Life Unfold

Now he uses us to spread the knowledge of Christ everywhere,
like a sweet perfume.
Our lives are a Christ-like fragrance rising up to God.
2 Corinthians 2:14-15 NLT

I am a June girl -- my birthday is in June, and I have always loved the traditional June flower, the rose. Yes, I especially adore pink or red roses. And their fragrance. O my!

So imagine my delight when my darling husband "showered me" with roses one year. First, a smiling delivery person, carrying a vase filled with perfectly formed hot pink roses framed in baby's breath, appeared on my doorstep. Next, a pop-up bouquet of cut-paper rose loveliness in a card was at my place at the table.

As if that wasn't enough, most special of all was John's message filled with scripture and poetic metaphor. It celebrated not only my love for roses, but my obsession with one of my favorite words – "unfolding." John had found the perfect message for my rose-laden birthday -- a poem, "Unfolding the Rose." But before I share the amazing poem, let me tell you about my beautiful word, "unfold."

"Let life unfold" was advice I had received years ago from my mentor friend Donna. She knew I was a "mover & shaker" type. At first it seemed hard to just let my days unfold. But as the years have passed, I have learned to rest in Christ. And so I don't find it as difficult as I used to. I've learned to "move and shake" more and more in the flow of the Spirit of Christ dwelling within.

So now every day in my journal, as the day is just beginning to "unfold," I write:

"Your unfolding fullness today, O Lord."

And I'm excited to see what my unfolding day entails. I often have things already on the "schedule." But then the next morning, I go back and list how the previous day had in reality unfolded. Usually nothing earthshaking, but at times truly amazing. It's exciting to note in writing what the Lord does day by day.

It reminds me of the proverb I had hanging on the wall in our nursery when our babies came along. And it is now in our guest room:

We make our plans, but God has the last word.
Proverbs 16:1 LB

Day by day, I declare,

"My Lord Jesus, You are my King.
Unfold Your fullness in and through me.
I serve at Your pleasure and for Your purpose today."
(See Acts 13:36)

So now for the poem that puts these two favorites together. As you read, may you be blessed and warmly inspired to embrace your life for the unfolding flower that it is. Our Master Gardener knows what He is about.

<u>Unfolding the Rose</u>

It is only a tiny rosebud,
A flower of God's design;
But I cannot unfold the petals
With these clumsy hands of mine.

The secret of unfolding flowers
Is not known to such as I.
GOD opens this flower so sweetly,
Then, in my hands, they die.

If I cannot unfold a rosebud,
This flower of God's design,
Then how can I have the wisdom
To unfold this life of mine?

So I'll trust in Him for leading
Each moment of my day.
I will look to Him for His guidance
Each step of the pilgrim way.

The pathway that lies before me,
Only my Heavenly Father knows.
I'll trust Him to unfold the moments,
Just as He unfolds the rose.
(Author Unknown)[8]

Brothers and sisters, He unfolds our days in ways we couldn't have imagined. Why not rest in Him and let Him do His work…beautifully. He is in control.

<u>Embrace Each Day</u>
You tell me to embrace each day
And let my life unfold.

Trusting that in every way
You are in control.

Not to rush into my plans
To faster reach my goal.

But to trust your perfect timing
And my future that You hold.
Penny Mandeville

<u>Prayer</u>
Lord of the unfolding rose, teach me to let You unfold my life in Your perfect way and in Your perfect timing. I'm such a mover and shaker at times. I know You live within and will move me along by Your Spirit. I am your vessel, your instrument, Your flower in Your world. Teach me to move with Your movement, letting You do the unfolding. In Jesus' Name. Amen.

<u>Reflections</u>
1. Are you trying to figure something out to fix it, to make it happen, to push through the "inertia" all around you. If possible, grab a rose, or at least, picture yourself trying to unfold the rose and make it bloom.

2. What is God telling you right now about your own life? Journal your conversation with Him about your life and how it is "unfolding" (or maybe staying "closed up.")

3. Here is the "back-story" to the poem: _https://bit.ly/3SgBMTO_

GLORY IN CHILDREN

Define yourself as one radically loved by God.[9]
Brennan Manning
Abba's Child

8. Pink Balls: Just Saying "YES"

Trust in the Lord with all your heart;
do not depend on your own understanding.
Seek his will in all you do,
and he will show you which path to take.
Proverbs 3:5-6 NLT

"Should we knock on the door or just leave them here?" I wasn't sure.

John and I were just passing through on our way home from a Bible conference at the Cove in Asheville, NC. And now we found ourselves on the front porch of a perfect stranger in a neighborhood of a city not our own.

Having checked into our hotel, we walked out the door to build up a few thousand steps on our exercise app. After all we had been sitting in the car for hours. And in the course of our walk, we found ourselves strolling past some houses in an older neighborhood -- reminiscent of earlier times in our lives.

Evidences of young families lay here and there -- a trampoline, toys, balls in yards. As we continued walking, we hadn't paid much attention to the young mom and three (or were there four?) little girls in a yard on the corner -- not until one by one, they greeted us with waves and sweet "hellos." One even came closer to make sure we noticed her too. So cute and kind. And the lovely mom was smiling. We returned their greetings and continued on our way, blessed by the preciousness of it all.

John and I decided to walk into the grocery store across from our hotel. We weren't needing anything in particular, just some more steps on our app (and to be out of the 90-degree heat).

And then I saw them — a big bin half-full of purple-y pink rubber balls … only pink. I had a quirky idea. "Why not buy four pink balls and take them back to those friendly little girls?" Could that be God? I told John the idea. It was then we recalled one of the significant messages we had heard at the conference just days before -- Jill Briscoe's message, "Just say Yes to God."

So we both said, "Yes, let's do it."

Back to the house, we walked. All was quiet. No one around. So there we were, standing on the front porch of perfect strangers in a neighborhood of a city not our own.

Should we knock?

Yes, knock!

The door opened. And fully arrayed in a Chewbacca costume stood "the Dad." His sweet little girls were all around as he answered the door to perfect strangers.

John was dumbfounded, but I just said to the dad, "We were walking past your house earlier, and your cute little girls greeted us enthusiastically. We thought they might enjoy these balls."

"Thank you's" resounded from the littles as we walked back down the driveway. And John and I went our way rejoicing, so glad that we had "just said Yes" to God.

What fun and what joy. What a "God-wink" those pink balls proved to be. It had seemed like a risk. But what risk? Life is too short to say "No" to God and miss the joy of being the vehicle of His love.

Is there something, dear friend, that seems a bit quirky, a bit scary, a bit risky? What do you have to lose? Step out and say, "Yes." Show up. Reach out. Buy that "pink ball" and take it to someone who may be delighted by your thoughtfulness.

Just say Yes. And experience His joy and pleasure.

And P.S. There <u>were</u> four, not three girls. Thank you, God.

Open My Eyes
Open my eyes,
And just show me who.

Open my ears.
Tell me what I should do.

Open my hands
To do something new.

Open their hearts
To see only You.
  Penny Mandeville

<u>Prayer</u>

O Lord of pink balls and precious girls. We could easily have missed the joyful delight of being Your instrument to love on that little family in that city not our own. Cause us to always hear you and just say "Yes."

We have nothing to lose and everything to gain -- experiencing the self-forgetful freedom of being the expresser of your indwelling life and love on this earth.

Thank you, in Jesus' name. Amen.

<u>Reflections</u>

Look around you today. Is there someone in your life who expects nothing from you, but whom you can secretly or surprisingly bless? For instance, since I've become a grandma, I've developed a reputation for my muffins. I began doing "muffin drops" at my grandchildren's house, usually "out of the blue." The kids know that every muffin represents a hug and a kiss. And we have even done "muffin drops" at friends' houses.

9. Morning Song: Waking Up Singing

Shout with joy to the Lord, all the earth!
Worship the Lord with gladness.
Come before him, singing with joy.
Psalm 100:1-2 NLT

What is it about two-year-olds? Do they all wake up singing? Or do we not notice that they do, until they don't? William and Claire, brother and sister (and our two youngest grandchildren) would wake up singing every morning when they were two years old. And each of them had their own unique repertoire.

William is the oldest. When he was two, William was our amazingly verbal comedian. And he would hit the ground running in the morning and keep it going till dropping into bed at night.

John and I visited often and stayed in their guest room when William was two. As I was barely awake one morning, I heard cheerful singing coming down the stairway from his bedroom into the guest room. It was William singing and singing. No one else was up in the household, just our little William, greeting the day with song.

Apparently, he did this most mornings, and his repertoire included "Mr. Golden Sun," "You are My Sunshine," and "Somewhere Over the Rainbow," with a smattering of "Tomorrow" and other songs added in. So precious. (But then my bubble burst one day when he woke up singing the "John Cena Wrestling song." Oh well.)

Years later when William's sweet sister Claire was two-years-old, she would also wake up with a song in her heart and on her lips. So then we were being awakened in the guest room by the sweet sounds of darling Claire's lilting voice.

But Claire's songs had a unique "dimension" to them. Although they were ones she had heard over and over again on her favorite show "Mother Goose Club," Claire often added a little twist. Claire's fun older brother Eli was often the subject of her songs.

For instance,

> Old MacDonald had a farm, ELI, ELI, O
> and on his farm he had a cow, ELI, ELI, O…

Another "unusual" one to hear spill out of the mouth of little Claire was

> Day-O, Day, -ay, -ay, -ay -O
> ELI come an' I wanna go home…

I still giggle, thinking about Claire and her big brother Eli.

And Claire makes me smile and think of my own Big Brother — not in my family of origin (I am the oldest of 7). No, I'm thinking of my Big Brother in the family of God, my Lord Jesus Christ.

We usually don't think of Jesus as our Brother, but what a precious truth this is. As our Brother, He understands and sympathizes because He became one of us — totally human. But He is also able to help and save to the uttermost because He is God — totally divine.

So now Jesus and the ones he makes holy have the same Father. That is why Jesus is not ashamed to call them his brothers and sisters…it was necessary for him to be made in every respect like us, his brothers and sisters, so that he could be our merciful and faithful High Priest before God. Then he could offer a sacrifice that would take away the sins of the people. Since he himself has gone through suffering and testing, he is able to help us when we are being tested.
Hebrews 2:13-18 NLT

And so I want Him to be the theme of all my songs as I walk out this life -- when I wake up and fall asleep at night and every moment in between.

May I ask you, dear friends, how do you wake up every day? Grumpy or grateful? And Who is the theme of the song of your life? Yourself or your Lord? Why not "sing" Him into every moment of your day?

<u>Morning Song</u>
As the birds sing with delight
In their morning chorus
Let's lift up our voices
To the One Who is for us.

Let's offer Him thanksgiving
For every new day
Acknowledging his presence
While unceasingly we pray.

Let's sing songs of love
And shower Him with praise.

And walk hand in hand with Him
Throughout all our days.
Penny Mandeville

<u>Prayer</u>
Lord, You are the Song of my life. Remind me from the moment I awaken to turn to You in praise and gratitude. And teach me to sing You, O my Jesus, into every moment of my day. In Your Sonshine-filled Name. Amen.

<u>Reflections</u>
1. Sing to the Lord first thing in the morning. Find your favorite hymn and sing it to the Lord as loud as you dare.

2. May I suggest going to the Bible's songbook, the book of Psalms. See what you can "beg, borrow, or steal" from the inspired singers of the faith. Psalms 100 and 103 are what I have gravitated toward. Notice how the psalmist exhorts his soul as well as all the earth (including "Mr. Golden Sun") to shout with joy and bless the Lord in worship.

3. My own morning song is "Be Thou My Vision." Through this beautiful, ancient song, I turn my thoughts early in my day to my Lord, my Savior, my Brother, Jesus Christ. I'll loan it to you (smile).

Be Thou my vision, O Lord of my heart
Naught be all else to me, save that Thou art
Thou my best thought, by day or by night
Waking or sleeping, Thy presence my light[10]
"Be Thou My Vision"
[Jan's morning song]

Morning has broken like the first morning
Blackbird has spoken like the first bird
Praise for the singing, praise for the morning
Praise for them springing fresh from the world[11]
"Morning Has Broken"
[Penny's grandmother's morning song]

10. Jesus Books: Learning from the "Littles"

But Jesus said, "Let the children come to me. Don't stop them!
For the Kingdom of Heaven belongs to those
who are like these children."
Matthew 19:14 NLT

Jesus books -- one of my most precious treasures. These little books date way back to our son Jeremy's and our daughter Beth's babyhoods. Little by little over the years, I added to the collection each time I stopped at the Christian bookstore, first in northern Virginia and then in Dallas.

These special books were handled and read with "enthusiasm." The contact paper covers couldn't hide the evidence of our babies' "love" for their "Jesus books" — chew marks and all.

Well, recently I rediscovered these treasures tucked away, long after Jeremy and Beth are grown and with children of their own. I wanted to replace them, but alas! They are out of print. So not long ago, I decided I would just take these original, worn but loved, "Jesus books" along on a visit to read with our youngest grandchildren.

Little did I know what a hit these treasures would be. Now visit after visit, the *Jesus books* appear, sometimes at rest time in the afternoon, sometimes at bedtime with nighttime prayers. Both William and Claire are "reading" them along with me. They take turns commenting and creating new scenarios that include themselves and those they love to go along with the pictures in the books.

The favorite Jesus book by far is *God is Always with Me.* What an important truth to sink down deep into their little minds and hearts … and ours also.

So I've taken the truth from each page and paired each one with meditations from the Scriptures for us "bigs" also. Maybe you can visualize your own scenarios that include you also (even without the pictures). I am so grateful for the deep, yet simple, truths that pour out of every page. They remind all of us that truly, "Jesus loves me, this I know."

God is with me when I'm by myself.

> You made all the delicate, inner parts of my body
> and knit me together in my mother's womb.
> Thank you for making me so wonderfully complex!
> Your workmanship is marvelous—how well I know it.
> You watched me as I was being formed in utter seclusion,
> as I was woven together in the dark of the womb.
> You saw me before I was born.
> Every day of my life was recorded in your book.
> Every moment was laid out
> before a single day had passed.
> Psalm 139:13-16 NLT

God is with me when there's a storm.

> When you go through deep waters,
> I will be with you.
> When you go through rivers of difficulty,
> you will not drown.
> When you walk through the fire of oppression,

you will not be burned up;
the flames will not consume you.
For I am the Lord, your God,
the Holy One of Israel, your Savior.
Isaiah 43: 2-3 NLT

<u>God is with me when it's dark.</u>

I will bless the Lord who guides me;
even at night my heart instructs me.
I know the Lord is always with me.
I will not be shaken, for he is right beside me.
Psalm 16:7-8 NLT

To you the night shines as bright as day.
Darkness and light are the same to you.
Psalm 139: 12b NLT

<u>God is with me when it's light.</u>

"I am the light of the world.
Whoever follows me will not walk in darkness,
but will have the light of life."
John 8:12 ESV

You will show me the way of life,
granting me the joy of your presence
and the pleasures of living with you forever.
Psalm 16:11 NLT

<u>God is with me when I'm lost.</u>

> I can never get away from your presence!
> If I go up to heaven, you are there;
> if I go down to the grave, you are there.
> If I ride the wings of the morning,
> if I dwell by the farthest oceans,
> even there your hand will guide me,
> and your strength will support me.
> Psalm 139:7b-10 NLT

<u>God is with me when I'm at home.</u>

> You see me when I travel
> and when I rest at home.
> You know everything I do.
> You know what I am going to say
> even before I say it, Lord.
> You go before me and follow me.
> You place your hand of blessing on my head.
> Psalm 139:3-4 NLT

<u>Thank you, God, for always being with me.</u>

> "… be sure of this: I am with you always, even to the end of the age."
> Matthew 28:20b NLT

<u>God is Always with Me</u>
Closer than a brother
Standing by my side

Closer than a Daddy
Giving a horsie ride

Closer than a mother
With a newborn at her breast

Closer still than these we are
And there my soul finds rest.
                Penny Mandeville

<u>Prayer</u>
Thank you, O my God, thank You for Your abiding Presence.
And thank You for my "littles" who lead me every time to Your
heart and the refreshment of Your Presence. I love how You said, ".
. . a little child shall lead them all."
Truth from Your Mouth to my ears. In Jesus' Name. Amen.

<u>Reflections</u>
1. Write out each of the statements from the little *Jesus Book* and
add your own verses to the collection. Visualize yourself in each.
Even draw your own pictures if you care to.
Thank your God for always being with you and your loved ones.

2. As an extra project, why not grab a good children's Bible
storybook. My absolute favorite is *The Jesus Storybook Bible: Every
Story Whispers His Name,* by Sally Lloyd-Jones.[12] It's a great one
for even us "bigs" to get an overview of God's story in the Bible,
especially seeing Jesus promised and present throughout.

11. The Coloring Book: Living Life in Color

The heavens proclaim the glory of God.
The skies display his craftsmanship.
Psalm 19:1 NLT

I have always loved to color. As a child, I looked forward to my new coloring book and crayons every Christmas. Years later as a mom, I loved coloring side by side with my daughter Beth and even now, with my granddaughter Claire.

Now that technology has entered the picture, I discovered with my grandsons a fun app called "Hidden Pictures." The best part of playing this matching game is when all the hidden items are matched up, the entire picture "colors up." Breathtaking.

All this coloring makes me think of God. Our God lives His life in color. All we need do is look around. Color is everywhere in creation – the golden sun, the blue sky, silvery dew on green grass, a yellow dandelion, multi-colored autumn leaves, and many glorious colors in His world around us.

And God's love of color is evident in people – in physical differences and even in feelings ("I feel blue"), ideas ("what a bright idea"), and circumstances ("the days are dark").

As Christians, who embrace a color-loving God, do we live our days "in color"? I'm not so sure we do. It seems we more often live in muted, shaded tones.

Why is that, I wonder?

I think we stay stuck in a partial view of the Gospel. We know Jesus, the Son of God, died for us to pay the penalty for our sins, so that we can go to heaven when we die. And we think that's all there is. So now we need to try to please God and get Him to love us and use us more. We need to live the way the Bible says Christians live.

So then we come up with our formulas and "to-do lists." The result is we live in a downward spiral of self-effort. We ask God for help, then more self-effort, followed by failure, bits of success, quickly followed by more failure. Then self- rejection so easily takes over.

Everything, even the joys and delights of life, get shaded with the grays and blacks of defeat. It all becomes muted and dull and heavy.

Our "self-efforting," religious activities obscure the glory of the new me, the new creation, indwelt by the Living Christ.

> This means that anyone who belongs to Christ has become a new person. The old life is gone; a new life has begun!
> 2 Corinthians 5:17 NLT

The gospel is about Life, God's Life. When we finally realize this truth — the living God living in us and through us, as us -- it's like being born again, again. Everything comes alive or *colors up.* Every day unfolds with fullness of color when we live from the life of Another, the Author of His own colorful Life, imparted to us.

But let's be honest. Sometimes the colors we encounter in life are gray or black, red or purple… the hard things of life. But even then, by faith we know that our glorious God is there all the time, within and all around, whether we see Him or not.

Brothers and sisters, how blessed we are to live not only in God's "Creation coloring book," but also and most importantly, in God's "New Creation coloring book" within. All because God loves us, His "colored-up kids." We are forgiven, but that's not all. We are alive with His fullness of Life.

Praise Him.

He Opened My Eyes
My life was weary and dreary
Like the sky before a storm.
I could see no beauty in it.
Only grey clouds were my norm.

Then the mighty storm hit
And tossed me around and more.
I almost lost the things I love.
I was shaken to my core.

When the storm passed I felt a peace
As grey clouds rolled away.
And I could see the brilliant colors
Of the world on display.

For in the storm the Lord
Opened my eyes to see His face
And now I see Him everywhere
And His beauty I embrace.
   Penny Mandeville

Prayer
Lord of all creation and new creation, we praise You. You are the One who enables us to live each day in Your Coloring Book -- not

just externally in Your physical creation, as glorious as that is, but also internally in our new self, indwelt by Your glorious Self. Teach us what it means to live "colored up" day by day in Your fullness. In Jesus' name. Amen.

<u>Reflections</u>
1. Dolly Parton sings a wonderful song called "God's Coloring Book."
Find Dolly's song on YouTube. Visualize or go out in nature and view what Dolly sings about in the song. How does that focus help you "color up" inside? What are you viewing in addition to what she saw? Can you write another stanza? Praise our colorful God.

> *And as I looked around me*
> *the more that I did look*
> *the more I realize that I am viewing*
> *God's coloring book*
> Dolly Parton, "God's Coloring Book"[13]

2. What "colors" might you be experiencing in your soul right now. Joy in circumstances, relationships? Sorrow? Both? Assign a color to each of your experiences.
Did you know there is a grace to "match" your trial? Every trial is a new opportunity to experience the grace of God:

> … you have been distressed by various [manifold, <u>multicolored</u>] <u>trials</u>, so that the proof of your faith, being more precious than gold which perishes though tested by fire, may be found to result in praise, glory, and honor at the revelation of Jesus Christ.
> 1 Peter 1:6 -7 NASB (emphasis, mine)

… the multifaceted [manifold, <u>multi-colored</u>] <u>grace</u> of God.
1 Peter 4:10b NASB (emphasis, mine)

3. Match your trial with His grace. Remember, from His fullness, we receive "*grace upon grace*." (John 1:16)
Someone has called this, "Grace Stacking."

12. The Frown: Choosing Your Face

Just as water mirrors your face, so your face mirrors your heart.
Proverbs 27:19, MSG

We chose our attitude.

I didn't always think that was true, but the older I get, the more I believe our choosing has a lot to do with it. I experienced this simple truth with a group of four-year-old's when I was teaching preschool years ago.

It was getting toward the end of the school year, maybe April or early May. I was reflecting on the precious group of "free spirits" entrusted to my care that year. The Lord had done some amazing spiritual work in the lives of those five four-year-old's and in my own life as their teacher.

But I was somewhat distressed, feeling that I hadn't quite "reached" one little boy. He usually looked stressed and often had a negative expression on his face -- a "NO" face. Somewhat resigned to the fact that "you can't win them all," I just kept on doing what we were doing.

One day, the children were washing their hands two by two. Little Johnny (not his real name) was not acting properly toward the child at the sink with him. So of course, I reprimanded him. Johnny glared at me with his "No" face, obviously not happy.

I said, "Johnny, don't give me that mean face. Give me a gentle face."

Immediately, he changed his face. Peace came over him. I was amazed.

About an hour later, we lined up by the door to go home. I took my usual place standing at the door facing the children. I waited until they formed a line in front of me. Then we would proceed down the hall and out to the waiting moms.

I looked at Johnny in line. He had his usual negative expression. But when we made eye contact, he immediately relaxed his expression and smiled.

Later, I asked the Lord about it. "Lord, what just happened?" He led me to an incredible Scripture I had never noticed before.

> A man's wisdom illumines him and causes his stern face to beam.
> Ecclesiastes 8:1 NASB

Days later, Johnny's mom came up to me and said, "Jan, you changed Johnny's life." She had seen a new peace in her child. And I praised God, knowing it wasn't me who made the change. It was the Holy Spirit working in one little boy's life, enabling him to "change his face."

Not long after, this same topic ran through discussion with a group of friends. One woman said she wanted to be more gentle. So the Lord led her to start closing doors and cabinets quietly. Another person wanted to not respond to mistakes in anger and frustration. So he began to speak out a gentle answer. He found it turned away his own wrath (Prov. 15:1).

After my husband's heart attack, John and I went to his cardiac rehab class called "The Emotional Side of Heart Disease." This was an excellent class about managing stresses, especially those associated with suffering a heart attack. We both looked at each other when the rehab nurse read an excerpt from an article called, "Laughter Really is the Best Medicine."[14]

> "Move joyfully. If you wake up in a bad mood, act like you're in a good mood, and your body can actually 'fake out' your own brain. It's called 'fake it till you make it.' When the copier breaks down in the office, instead of hitting it, try twirling while you tell people the copier isn't working. Trust me, when you do this, it's impossible to feel stressed. By substituting playful gestures for angry ones, your brain often short-circuits your own stress."

I'm not so sure I can see my engineer husband twirling at the copier. But this principle is at the heart of the way the body and mind work together.

But even better news for us believers is we have the mind of Christ. So we can choose to yield our body to Him and His indwelling life. We can "choose our face" and expect that His empowering, indwelling Life will live through us for His glory.

So, dear brothers and sisters, "choose your face and change your day." And ultimately, let it can change the way you live your life in this world…to the glory of God…one day at a time.

> …we have the mind of Christ.   1 Corinthians 2:16b NASB

<u>Make Me Smile</u>
Turn Your countenance upon me
And change my worried face.

May I look upon this troubled world
As You do -with all grace.

There must be many things that You
Would like to see erased.

You love us so and want to see
Our misery replaced.

But how sublime, one smile at a time
You change the human race.
                    Penny Mandeville

 <u>Prayer</u>
Lord, thank You that I have Your mind, and I also have Your indwelling Spirit.   Remind me each day that I have a choice how I will respond to situations and people that come my way. May my face reflect Yours. I choose You. Teach me and change me. Amen.

<u>Reflections</u>
Meditate on this Scripture. Ask the Holy Spirit to remind you that you chose your attitude each day. And you can start by choosing your face.

> Have this attitude in yourselves which was also in Christ Jesus, who, although He existed in the form of God, did not regard equality with God a thing to be grasped, but emptied Himself, taking the form of a bond-servant, and being made

in the likeness of men. Being found in appearance as a man, He humbled Himself by becoming obedient to the point of death, even death on a cross. Philippians 2:5-8, NASB

13. The Blessing: Giving and Receiving

He was still speaking when,
behold, a bright cloud overshadowed them,
and a voice from the cloud said,
"This is my beloved Son, with whom I am well pleased;
listen to him."
Matthew 17:5 ESV

The letter to the Hebrews is one of my favorite books in the New Testament. One time, when I was making my way through Hebrews 11, I read as if for the first time about two patriarchs, Isaac and Jacob.

By faith Isaac blessed Jacob and Esau in regard to their future. By faith Jacob, when he was dying, blessed each of Joseph's sons, and worshiped as he leaned on the top of his staff.   Hebrews 11:20-21 NIV

It wasn't the key word "faith" that caught my attention, but the word "blessed." By faith, these "patriarch - dads" blessed their sons.

Years before, I had read *The Blessing* by Gary Smalley & John Trent.[15] In that wonderful book, the authors explore our human need for approval and validation. They explained how the biblical blessing of fathers to their children met this need. And they also shared how we could do this for our children and for others we care about today.

The authors listed 5 elements to the Blessing:
- Meaningful touch
- Spoken words

- Expressing High value
- Picturing a Special Future
- Active commitment

I intended to use what I learned from this book to bless my own young adult children and the ladies in my Bible study group. I basically left it at that, but God had other ideas.

I was teaching a small preschool class of five precious four-year-old's. We bonded throughout that school year. Now it was the last day of school. We went through a lot together that year -- field trips, singing, snacks, crafts, counting, bible stories, reading books, puzzles, and lots more. And now the end -- always a mixture of sadness and nostalgia and loss. It meant saying "good-bye" to this sweet group of little persons, nevermore under my "tutelage."

So at the end of class that day, each child gathered his things in his appointed box for the last time. We were all lined up and starting to walk down the hall when the Holy Spirit stopped me.

"Bless them."

"Bless them?"

"Bless them."

So there in the hallway, I laid my hands on each of those sweet children, one by one. I prayed over each in turn -- unique words and blessings for every child. I was in tears.

But what I'll never forget were the eager little faces. They were like little birds with their mouths open wide to receive. Each child was waiting his turn to be blessed. No dry eyes for me. And I learned the value of blessing others.

We may not have received the needed blessing of affirmation from our own dads. No matter. We can and actually, must receive it from our Heavenly Father.

> Blessed be the God and Father of our Lord Jesus Christ, who has blessed us in Christ with every spiritual blessing in the heavenly places … Ephesians 1:3 ESV

And then the amazing and wonderful thing is we can be our Father God's instrument of blessing to others. We can be His voice of affirmation and hope, His hug of love and tenderness, and His tears of joy and delight.

Friends, is there someone in your life that needs love and affirmation? Hope and encouragement? Why not speak a blessing ... and be a blessing.

<u>Bless My Friend</u>
Dear Lord, when I ask you to bless my friend
May you show them your favor and grace without end.
May You lead them and make their path straight without bend.
May You make them aware of Your presence and then
Protect them and guide them toward You till the end.
Penny Mandeville

<u>Prayer</u>
O Abba Father God, Lover of heart and soul. You have blessed me abundantly with Your unconditional love and acceptance and grace. You have healed my soul of the many lies I have believed about

Who You are and Your attitude toward me.

Now in Your mercy and abundance, may I be Your instrument to speak blessing into the lives of those who so desperately need to hear from You, their Loving Creator Father God.

In Jesus' Name. Amen.

<u>Reflections</u>

1. There are many opportunities to bless others. Children and adults ("children incognito") are hungry for our Father God's blessing – through you and me.

Watch for the opportunities God sends your way. And then step out in faith -- open your mouth, and say those life affirming words someone may be longing to hear.

Write that note, send that text or email. Communicate what the Lord gives you for that precious person whom He loves. Speak a blessing. Be the blessing.

2. My dear neighbor and friend Jackie describes the "Blessing of Children" at her church:

> We practice and teach weekly blessings of God, offered to children in a time of prayer and blessing. After prayer, there is a blessing of God offered to each child, by name.

> *"__________, God created you. God loves you.*
> *God is with you, God blesses you - to be a blessing."*

> Then, we offer a tangible example of God's blessings, by marking a sign of the cross on the hand or arm of the person.

> *"Go and be a blessing, dear __________."*

> Jackie Nowak, Founder, *The Blessing Center Collaborative*

GLORY IN QUIET

Christian rest is <u>not</u> inactivity.
Christian rest is rest
because He carries the load.[16]
Major W. Ian Thomas,
The Indwelling Life of Christ

14. The Prayer Chair: Being Held

Don't worry about anything; instead, pray about everything.
Tell God what you need, and thank him for all he has done.
Then you will experience God's peace,
which exceeds anything we can understand.
His peace will guard your hearts and minds
as you live in Christ Jesus.
Philippians 4:6-7 NLT

I have a new chair. I call it my prayer chair.

For years I had a comfortable chair in a little corner where I prayed and meditated and read the Word. It was deep down in the inner sanctum of the house where nobody goes. But I never thought of it as my prayer chair. It was a family heirloom belonging to my mother-in-law.

When our daughter Beth moved into a new home, she had the perfect place for the chair. So the green, comfy chair, belonging to Beth's grandma, went to her perfect spot in the corner of the family room in her new home. I was thrilled for Beth and for the chair. It was staying in the family and was being loved.

But what to put in its place? Of course. The rocking chair that I had rocked my babies in years ago. I love that chair. But somehow it wasn't the same —not because it wasn't special. It certainly was. But it just didn't work in my little corner. And being wooden, it wasn't working for my aging bones.

But then, I saw her, in all her white, leathery, puffy and comfy glory, there in the back room of my favorite consignment shop in my favorite little town...my new-to-me "prayer chair." I wasn't even looking for her. I was just browsing in that favorite shop in that favorite town. And there she was. At the time, I hadn't even recognized her as my prayer chair. But as the days went by, I couldn't get the chair out of my mind. God had "given" me my chair.

So we went to pick up my treasure and place her in her new home. And morning by morning, with coffee mug in hand, Bible in lap, and journal opened to today, I rest in my "cloud" of a chair and commune with my Lord.

But why all this joy in a chair in a remote corner of my house? Several reasons, I think. My little corner means I'm alone...alone with my Maker. So I can "be still and know that He is God," and I'm not. But He is my Father, and I'm His beloved daughter.

> See how great a love the Father has bestowed on us, that we would be called children of God; and such we are.
> 1 John 3:1 NASB

My chair says "Rest" to my soul. So I respond to Jesus' words,

> Come to me, all of you who are weary and carry heavy burdens, and I will give you rest. Take my yoke upon you. Let me teach you, because I am humble and gentle at heart, and you will find rest for your souls. For my yoke is easy to bear, and the burden I give you is light.
> Matthew 11:28-30 NLT

My cloud of a chair reminds me of my helplessness, my neediness for Him.

> Humble yourselves, therefore, under the mighty hand of
> God so that at the proper time he may exalt you, casting all
> your anxieties on him, because he cares for you.
> 1 Peter 5:6-7 ESV

As I sink down into the softness of my prayer chair, I am assured
that He is the Strong One. He holds me in my weakness.

> "My grace is all you need. My power works best in
> weakness." So now I am glad to boast about my
> weaknesses, so that the power of Christ can work through
> me. That's why I take pleasure in my weaknesses, and in the
> insults, hardships, persecutions, and troubles that I suffer for
> Christ. For when I am weak, then I am strong.
> 2 Corinthians 12:9-10 NLT

As one author says,

> The indispensable condition for developing and maintaining
> the awareness of our beloved-ness is time alone with God. In
> solitude we tune out the naysaying whisper of our
> worthlessness and sink down into the mystery of our true
> self.[17]

What about you, my friend? Do you have a special place, a beloved
chair or other piece of furniture? I highly recommend it. Nothing
compares with meeting with your God in a quiet place, sharing your
burdens and hearing His thoughts, praying for loved ones and even
those who are hard to love. So why not...

Let Him love you and hold you, dear one, in your quiet place...today
and every day.

<u>Our Special Place</u>
Take me to our special place
Where we can be alone.

Remind me of the things You've done
That only we have known.

Calm my soul and give to me
A listening ear to hear.

I see your face, Your love and grace
Which cast out every fear.

You fill me with assurance
You'll hear my every prayer

So when I despair I'll meet you there
In that place that's ours to share.
           Penny Mandeville

<u>Prayer</u>
Lord, You Yourself are my place of peace and rest. I'm so glad that I can commune with You anywhere at any time. I don't really need a physical place, because You are my place. But I do thank You for the gift of my special place. There we meet together alone, shutting the door to all that would distract. And thank You for my chair that reminds me I am held in Your embrace. I love You, my Lord, and I love our time together. Amen.

<u>Reflections</u>
1. Do you have a special place where you can go to meet with the

Lover of your Soul? If not, ask the Lord and see where He may point out to you.

2. If you already have a place, enjoy your Lord there today. Meditate on the scriptures shared in this devotion. Journal your thoughts and prayers.

3. If you cannot have a regular place because of circumstances beyond your control, don't feel guilty. The Lord indwells you by His Holy Spirit. (See the next meditation). You can commune with Him any time, any place. Thank Him for this and enjoy Him right where you are.

15. Anywhere: Communing in the Secret Place

But you belong to God, my dear children…
the Spirit who lives in you is greater
than the spirit who lives in the world.
1 John 4:4 NLT

Where do you go to commune with your God?

Do you go to a chapel or a church? To a favorite place near a stream, at a mountain retreat, or on a beach? Do you go to a "prayer closet," a special place in your own home, like my "prayer chair"?

Or maybe you are frustrated because there never seems to be a time and a "place" where you can go. Maybe you're a mom with young children or a special needs child. Perhaps you are a working mom or a worker who needs to moonlight at a second job to make ends meet. Maybe you or a loved one has a handicap or serious illness that takes you to medical places that seem to consume your life. Where is the place for you?

I have good news for all of us who know God through His Son, our Lord Jesus Christ. We have a place where we can go...at any time, at any place, without special clothing, without travel, without special access, without expense, without religious paraphernalia, without anything. Only our eternal souls, beloved by our God and united to Him in the deepest of the deep. The place of spirit-union with Him.

Can I tell you about how I began to learn about this place of communion, this "deep place where nobody goes"[18] or can go?

It was at a very dark time in our family. Our twenty-year old son had just walked through the trial of his young life of faith. He had been diagnosed with cancer in February of that year. After a long surgery and a radioactive iodine treatment, Jeremy was cancer free. We were elated and exhausted. All I can say is God carried us through. And His Presence was almost tangible.

But then about a month later, our sixteen-year-old daughter came to us with the scary news of having found several lumps. We went to the oncologist. He determined they were indeed tumors, but a "wait and see" strategy for a couple months would be wise. The tumors could be benign and shrink on their own. And so we waited. And that's when intense darkness descended upon this mama's soul. The "waiting game" was a killer.

One dark morning, I was on my way to teach my preschool class. The horrific possibility of having two children with cancer was obsessing my mind. My conversation with the Lord went like this:

> "Lord, how can this be happening? How can we have two children with cancer? What kind of toxic waste-dump have we been living in?"

After more struggle and questioning, God assured me that He was doing a work in our lives. I replied,

> "I trust you are doing something, Lord, and I don't have to understand it all. But how, as Mom, do I make it through?"

Clear as a bell in the darkness of the pre-dawn, the Holy Spirit spoke to my heart,

"Go to the place where you and I live together and nothing
can touch."

Not cancer, not the darkness, not people, not circumstances,
nothing.

Even though I didn't totally understand, I went there -- to that deep
inner place of soul/spirit union with my God. And there I
experienced "the peace that passes understanding. "

But when I began once again to look at the darkness and upheaval
all around, I would go back into turmoil. I had chosen to go back to
the "surface place where everyone lives."[18]

I made it through the back-and-forth action of my soul...deep place
of peace, then surface place of turmoil...back and forth, but all the
while I was learning. Thankfully, Beth didn't have cancer. But
through it all, God revealed Himself to me in the secret place.

Over the years since that hard lesson, I have learned to go day by
day to that secret place where God and I live together. I don't have to
be in any special geographic place. Although I love my beach days
of communion with God, those days are rare. But my times of
communion with my God are every day, any time of the day or night
and any place at all.

And they are for you too, my dear sisters and brothers. Go to the
"secret place" where you live together with your God. Go to the
deep place where no one else can go and nothing that comes at you
can touch. Then you and I can go out to the surface place where
everyone lives. We can bring the fullness of Christ who lives in us

to the people and circumstances all around us each day.

<u>My Heart—His Sanctuary</u>
I carry with me in my heart
The sanctuary of the Lord.

I worship and I praise Him there
And listen to His Voice.

His Word cuts through confusion
Just like a two edged sword.

I can feel His peace around me
And I know I am adored.

His presence is so real to me
That it cannot be ignored.

For His overflowing love and peace
Into my life He's poured.

I meet the Holy Spirit there
And oh! How my Spirit soars.

How thankful I am to know once again
That He's my heavenly source.
        Penny Mandeville

<u>Prayer</u>
Indwelling Lord God, Savior of my life, thank You that I can run to
You in my darkness and in my light because You are always there in
the inner sanctum of my spirit. Woo me, draw me, remind me where

to go in my experiences of life. I am so prone to forget and treat you as if You are "out there somewhere." I embrace You as You are embracing me—in the secret place. In Jesus' name. Amen.

<u>Reflections</u>

1. Spend some time today, visualizing that place deep in your spirit where only you and the Lord live. Rest there. Commune with Him there. Speak words of love and adoration to the One who is in union with you there at all times.

2. Ask the Holy Spirit to remind you of His Abiding Presence in that Secret Place where nobody else can go and nothing else can touch. Then go out into your day filled with the sense of His Presence.

3. Journal your experience.

16. The Nap: Longing for Rest

Come to me, all who labor and are heavy laden,
and I will give you rest…
Matthew 11:28 ESV

Ah! Rest...what a glorious word. I remember as a mom of an infant how I longed for rest, praying that my crying-in-the-middle-of-the-night baby would just fall quietly back to dreamland. Or my napping toddler would stay napping so I could lie prostrate for just a few more moments (Please, God).

And oh, how we all need deep, glorious rest. Not just moms need it; dads do too. Single folk need it; workers need it; and even kids need it (although they would protest most loudly...especially in the midst of the frenetic-ness of no-sleep sleepovers).

And now even as a senior retired adult, that beautiful rest calls my name in the midst of my afternoons. So I often take to my overstuffed couch and doze as I watch the old westerns from my childhood.

I think our craving for physical rest is just a picture of the rest we need even more for our souls. That's why Christ's invitation is so attractive. We see it here:

> Come to me, all who labor and are heavy laden, and I will give you rest. Take my yoke upon you, and learn from me, for I am gentle and lowly in heart, and you will find rest for your souls. For my yoke is easy and my burden is light.
> Matthew 11:28-30 ESV

Here in the gospel of Matthew, Jesus promises rest as a gift. This is not just the "take a nap" kind of rest. It goes much deeper. It is "inner tranquility" even while "engaged in necessary labor."

In our passage, we see Jesus teaching and preaching to a crowd of people in Galilee. These people would include His disciples, who were His learners. The religious leaders dogged His every step, so of course, they surely were part of this crowd. But in the previous verses, there is a hint at who Jesus' real audience is. Listen to how He prayed just before His invitation.

> At that time Jesus declared, "I thank you, Father, Lord of heaven and earth, that you have hidden these things from the wise and understanding and revealed them to little children; yes, Father, for such was your gracious will. All things have been handed over to me by my Father, and no one knows the Son except the Father, and no one knows the Father except the Son and anyone to whom the Son chooses to reveal him. Come to me, all who labor and are heavy laden, and I will give you rest…
> Matthew 11:25-28 ESV

Jesus' primary offer was to the common folk, like you and me. We are "ragamuffins," as one author calls us. Not the "perfect people" who have it all together. No, it's for those of us who know we don't have it together. Maybe we keep on trying. We are the "weary ones" who work our religious "to do list" to exhaustion. Or we are the "heavy laden," burdened by the failure of falling back into habits of sinful shame. The invitation is for all of us who know we need something we cannot produce. So we see and hear Jesus, with His beautiful "yes face," call to us,

"Come to Me, all you who are weary and heavy laden, and I will give you rest …"

Literally, it reads,

"Here to Me, and I will rest you."

Wow! Our Lord is pointing to Himself as the Person who is the place of rest. He is unlike the Pharisees who were following Him and harassing the people with their "religious mega-list."

And this inner rest of spirit that Jesus gives as a gift is the rest of union with Him (Colossians 3:3). This is rest indeed. And this rest is fixed, permanent, unchanging. It includes total forgiveness of all our sins, past, present, and future (Ephesians 1:7; Hebrews 10:17; 2 Corinthians 5:17); birth into God's family as a beloved child of God (John 1:12; 1 John 3:1-2); identification with Christ in death, burial, and resurrection (Romans 6:4-14; Galatians 2:20). It means Christ is living in me by His Holy Spirit (Colossians 1:27; 1 Corinthians 6:17,19). I have all of Him in all of me (Colossians 2:9-10). And this is true the moment I respond to Christ's invitation: "Here … to ME."

He rests me.

So there is no more working, no earning, no trying to be right in God's eyes; no grasping for His love; no agonizing over getting more of Him and His Spirit. I have it all because I have Him. It's all about receiving Him who is my promised Sabbath Rest.

So may I ask you, dear brother and sister in Christ, are you resting in Him who is your Rest? Or are you still trying to achieve what you already have and who you already are in Him? Let it all go and hear Christ's invitation,

Here . . .to Me.

Trust and Rest
Whether mighty warrior or lovely maiden
We all at times feel heavy laden
With the cares and the fears of this world.
Peace seems unattainable
But is available and sustainable
As we trust and rest in the Lord.
        Penny Mandeville

Prayer
Lord Jesus, You Yourself are my rest now and forever. Teach me to relinquish my striving to You and receive from Your gracious hand what only You could provide – inner tranquility of mind and heart no matter the circumstance I face. In your Name. Amen.

Reflections
1. Search out the statements and Scriptures above. Write them out in your journal and meditate. Then enjoy the rest that He has promised. Sink down deep into Him who rests in you.

2. Meditate on this version:

> Are you tired? Worn out? Burned out on religion? Come to me. Get away with me and you'll recover your life. I'll show you how to take a real rest. Walk with me and work with me—watch how I do it. Learn the unforced rhythms of grace. I won't lay anything heavy or ill-fitting on you. Keep

company with me and you'll learn to live freely and lightly.
Matthew 11:28-30 MSG

17. Worker Bee: Resting While You Work

Take my yoke upon you, and learn from me,
for I am gentle and lowly in heart,
and you will find rest for your souls.
Matthew 11:29-30 ESV

I've always been a doer—well, maybe not as a kid. But as an adult and, especially as a Christian adult woman; yes, I've been a worker-bee. I get the greatest pleasure in life by accomplishing a goal. But a driven-ness can take over in this way of living.

And I've discovered that being a worker-bee is especially dangerous when it comes to the spiritual life. I've lived for a long time under the yoke of what I call "to do list" Christianity. What a bondage. Self-effort doesn't work when it comes to doing what only God can do -- which is anything and everything of any spiritual value. That's why I love the Lord's invitation to the weary, burdened folk who followed Him:

> Come to me, all who labor and are heavy laden, and I will give you rest. Take my yoke upon you, and learn from me, for I am gentle and lowly in heart, and you will find rest for your souls. For my yoke is easy, and my burden is light. Matthew 11:28-30 ESV

Christ's invitation is a call to find true rest in Him alone. And this rest is a gift (literally, "I will rest you"). It's the rest of spirit that is fixed and permanent, resulting from all that the Person and Work of Christ accomplished for us – total forgiveness, birth into the family of God, union with Christ, and much more. And this rest of spirit is mine when I respond to Jesus' gracious words, "Here to Me" (verse 28).

But now the question is how do I experience this rest in my soul every day of my life on this earth? How can rest be mine even in the midst of all the "doing what needs to be done"? How can "the inner tranquility of soul while engaged in our necessary labors" be mine right here, right now? I believe it's all wrapped up in the image of the yoke.

A yoke is a bar or frame of wood that connects two animals together for a purpose or work of some kind. This was and is a common sight in the Middle East. Typically, a stronger animal is yoked to a weaker or more inexperienced one and so takes the lead. The two animals then work together to complete the same job. Symbolically, the yoke is a picture of being attached to one who is stronger and more skilled to accomplish a purpose together.

Jesus says that I am to take on His yoke in order to find rest for my *soul*. My soul is my inner person – my mind, my emotions, and my will. And this is where I often struggle and experience lack of peace and rest. But as I chose living from union with HIM above all other competing attachments, I experience the peace and rest of a Loving Lord who lives through me in every situation I face.

However, the fact is that there are other yokes pulling at me. These other attachments are often good things. But they often end up becoming addictions, obsessions, dependencies, mini-gods that exert control over my life. Christine Wyrtzen, in her lovely website *Daughters of Promise,* names a few we can become attached to if we are not yoked to Him above all else:

- the yoke of *religion* and living by "others' measuring stick" (like the Pharisees of Jesus' day)
- the yoke of *slavery* and living by "the demands of controllers"
- the yoke of *shame* and living by "the opinions of flawed people"
- the yoke of the *flesh* and living "like I did before I believed"
- the yoke of *deception* and living by "lies conceived at the gates of darkness."[19]

And I might add …

- the yoke of *self-effort* and living by my own ingenuity and type-A personality

But as I take His *yoke* upon me, as I yield to the loving Lord who lives within me, I experience what Major Ian Thomas calls the *faith-rest life*:

> …Christ is in action, and you in your humanity are simply the clothes of His divine activity. This is the rest of faith…it is your hands with which He is at work, your lips with which He is speaking, your eyes with which He sees the need, your ears with which He hears the cry, and your heart with which He loves the lost.[20]

So dear brothers and sisters, "take His yoke upon you" today and live from His indwelling life—as you are preparing the next meal, running to that necessary appointment, heading off to the workplace, cleaning up that spill, reading the Scriptures, loving your spouse, juggling job responsibilities, making that business call, changing another diaper, speaking the truth in love, refereeing the latest sibling squabble, helping with homework, comforting a hurting friend -- whatever unfolds before you each day. And you may be surprised to experience…

- Love beyond your love
- Forgiveness beyond your forgiveness
- Patience beyond your patience
- Skill beyond your skill
- Fullness beyond your fullness
- Peace beyond your peace
- Rest beyond your rest.

And you may also discover that His yoke is easy and His burden is light, because you are united to Him. And His yoke for you fits you perfectly.

<u>Yoked to Jesus</u>
With whom am I yoked?
By whom am I taught?
At the end of my life
Will it all be for naught?

If it's Jesus I'm yoked to
The power is His might.
Then my labor is easy
My burden is light.

The outcome doesn't
Depend on me.
For His work
Lasts for eternity.
      Penny Mandeville

<u>Prayer</u>

Lord Jesus, I chose You and Your yoke above all the others vying for my attention and my affection. Open my eyes to see where we are going and what we are doing together. I live from my rest in union with You, my only Lord and Master. In Your Name. Amen.

<u>Reflections</u>

Make your usual "to do list"/ schedule for your day. Be sure to include some blanks. Then go to the Lord with your list. Yield the list to the Lord. Let Him, as the day goes on, fill in the blanks, cross off what is not yours to do with Him, and check what is yours to do together.

18. Job Description: Abiding in Him

By this My Father is glorified, that you bear much fruit,
and so prove to be My disciples.
John 15:8 ESV

Have you ever started a job with no job description? I have, and it's pretty confusing.

Years ago, I was looking for a part-time teaching job. A friend asked if I would like to apply to substitute teach in ESOL & GED classes. I told her I didn't have a clue about either one. She assured me that it wasn't difficult. All I had to do was follow the teacher's lesson plans. So I naively applied.

Well, just as my application reached the supervisor's desk, the beginning level ESOL teacher was in a serious automobile accident. This was at the end of the first week of class. By then, beginning students don't know much more English than the day they walked in. On top of that, the injured teacher had no lesson plans and no curriculum. She was so experienced she did her own "curriculum." Needless to say, I was terrified.

So that entire first year, I had no job description. I just took the bull by the horns and prayed and taught and loved it. And I think the students did too, by God's grace. God more than abundantly met me in my need. And I taught that class for 9 more years.

However, without a job description, I made many mistakes and got myself in trouble more than once. Most of the time, my mistakes

were from my ignorance or from my zeal to "do things right." As a
result, I unknowingly went over my supervisor's head. Not good.

And that's what, I think, happens for us believers with living the
Christian life. We don't understand our "job description." We try
to do in our own strength what only God can do.

The Gospel of John, Chapter 15 is a perfect place to see what it
means to be a Christian (the branches) in relation to our Father (the
Owner/Gardener) and His Son (the True Vine).

So let's look at who does what in a vineyard.

First, the Gardener or Vinedresser. His job is to care for the vine
and branches by watering, fertilizing, and above all, pruning.
Without that almost "violent" pruning, a rich crop cannot come
forth.

And after all, the vineyard owner's reputation is at stake. If someone
sees a barren vineyard, no one shames the branches or even the vine,
but rather the gardener. That's because whoever does the work gets
the credit or the blame.   So it's his job to do whatever is necessary
to ensure an abundant crop of grapes. Even the good, new growth
gets cut back so as to bring forth an abundance of fruit.

> …My Father is the vinedresser…and every branch that bears
> fruit, He prunes it so that it may bear more fruit.
> John 15:1-2 NASB

This is what the Father does for us branches. Sometimes we may
feel like we've grown so much and have been "fruitful"...then all of a

sudden, the desert, dryness, seeming barrenness. But the process is not done yet.

Then there's the Vine. The Vine is the source of life for the branches. Without the life of the Vine flowing through healthy branches, nothing fruitful can come forth. Jesus is the Source of life for us, His branches.

> In Him was life, and the life is the light of men...I came that they might have life, and have it abundantly.
> John 1:4; 10:10b NASB

And that's why the main job of the Branches is to abide or live connected to the Vine. The branches are the vehicles for the life of the Vine to flow through so that fruit will come forth. Jesus said,

> "Abide in Me and I in you. As the branch cannot bear fruit of itself, unless it abides in the vine, so neither can you, unless you abide in Me."   John 15:4 NASB

So what does it mean *to abide* in Christ? It means to live in & from, remain in, sink down deep into, rest in, stay [experientially] connected to Christ, the Vine. We already "abide/live in Him" through our union with Christ. But we experience the fruitfulness of abiding when we walk through our daily life depending on Him.

Here's a feeble, but I hope helpful, illustration of what I think it means to abide. I have this wonderful couch in my living room. It is hard to sit or lie on this couch without falling asleep. When I used to come home from a full day of teaching, I would look forward to sinking my weary body into that couch. I would often just put on some instrumental music and surrender to the comfort of my glorious couch. Later, I'd leave that place refreshed and energized.

However, sometimes I still had things I needed to do before supper time. So I would abandon my tired self to my life-giving couch. But then I would make my phone calls or read my lessons or do whatever duty or desire dictated. I still came away refreshed because I was working from a position of rest, "abiding."

That's what I think abiding in Christ means. I do what I do from my position of rest in my Glorious Vine. I'm secure in Him and He in me. I am securely attached to Him forever. His resurrection life flows through me, His branch, to bring forth the fruit designed by the Father for my unique life.

What about you? Are you living the Branch-life? Do you do what you do from the position of rest in your Glorious Lord Christ? Or are you trying to do in your own strength and ingenuity what only God can do -- give life and produce fruit?

<u>Fruit That Will Last</u>
I can grunt and groan
And complain and moan
And struggle to produce some fruit.

But I learn very fast
That my fruit won't last
For it's not connected to the root.

So, I'm clinging to You
For all that I do.
I can never do it alone.

But from a place of rest
Snuggled into your chest
I will do what you condone.

When with you I abide
It's You who provides
The fruit that will truly fulfill

There's no job more precious
No reward of treasures
Can compare with doing your will.
      Penny Mandeville

Prayer

Lord, You are the Vine. I am Your beloved branch. And that is all I ever have to be. Teach me to abide, to rest in Who You are in me. Save me from my fleshly tendency to try to do by my self-effort what only You can do – produce fruit to the glory of the Father.

Reflections

1. Make a list from your own life of what you think is God the Gardener's job, Jesus the Vine's job, and you the branch's job.

2. Reread the devotional again and ask the Lord if you need to revise your list. Surrender all to Him.

3. Spend some time with this thought:

"You are the branch—You need be nothing more.

You need not for one single moment of the day take upon you the
responsibility of the Vine.
You need not leave the place of entire dependence
and unbounded confidence."[21]
Andrew Murray, *The True Vine*

GLORY IN RELATIONSHIPS

You are what you love.[22]
James KA Smith

19. Romance: Loving Jesus

I have loved you with an everlasting love;
therefore, I have continued my faithfulness to you.
Jeremiah 31:3 ESV

When my husband John and I were seniors at the University of Arizona, the *Carpenters* were at the top of the music charts.   We embraced them as "our group" who sang "our songs" as we were "a-courting." Their mellow sound and rich melodies fed our romantic feelings toward each other and toward life in general.

At our wedding, we danced to, you may have guessed it, "We've Only Just Begun." Lyrics like "White lace and promises, a kiss for luck and we're on our way" made it the perfect song to start our new marriage. Or so we thought. But years have rolled by and reality has set in. We have come to realize only an Almighty God could fulfill those unrealistic expectations.

The wonderful thing is with growth in Christ we learn to let our mate "off the hook." We let go of those expectations. So our spouse can be human and not so god-like. We learn to forgive and then receive everything as a free gift. We recognize God as our ultimate Source of life and love.

But what about all those love songs? Lest you think me cynical and jaded, I have to say they are valid within reason. But there came a time in my life, when I began to really listen to the words. It was then I realized the only One I could honestly sing them to is my Lord Jesus, the perfect Son of God.

And the song that opened my eyes to that truth was a favorite of ours, "I Won't Last a Day Without You." Here is the chorus to that heart-grabbing song.

> *When there's no getting over that rainbow*
> *When my smallest of dreams won't come true*
> *I can take all the madness the world has to give*
> *But I won't last a day without you.*[23]

The only One we can never live without is our Lord. Loved ones, including spouses, are gifts. But we will lose them through death or life changes. The Lover of our Soul will never leave us. He never changes. He is the Only One who can see us through.

<u>Your Love</u>
There's a hunger inside me I've tried to fulfill
By pleasing the world and by doing its will.

I've filled up with food and with lovely possessions
And relationships in which I've made unhealthy concessions.

I've tried to please others to be accepted by them
To the point I've lost track of just who I am.

Eventually I recognize the futility of my delusion
And with Your help, Lord, I have come to the conclusion

That there's only one love that makes me feel whole
One love that can satisfy my spirit and soul.

It's Your love that You willingly pour out on me
Because You love me absolutely unconditionally.
    Penny Mandeville

<u>Prayer.</u>
I love YOU, my Father.
I love YOU, my Jesus.
I love YOU, my Spirit of Life.

<u>Reflections</u>
1. The song that gave me that first "aha" moment many years ago was "I Won't Last a Day Without You." Would you like to join me in singing it from the heart to the Lover of your soul and mine? Pull it up on YouTube. Listen closely to the lyrics. Then sing it to your God.

2. Here are some other love songs to look at and sing:

"Through the Years," Kenny Rogers

> *Through the years, you've never let me down*
> *You turned my life around, the sweetest days I've*
> *found*
> *I've found with you... Through the years*
> *I've never been afraid, I've loved the life we've made*
> *And I'm so glad I've stayed, right here with you*
> *Through the years.*[24]

"Annie's Song," Travis Cottrell

> *You fill up my senses*
> *Like a night in a forest*
> *Like the mountains in springtime*
> *Like a walk in the rain*
> *Like a storm in the desert*

Like a sleepy blue ocean
You fill up my senses
Come fill me again.[25]

What's your favorite love song? Sing it to the Lover of your Soul.
Loving Jesus will heal your soul.

3. Read through the Bible's songbooks, the Psalms and the Song of Solomon. Copy into your journal the loving lyrics of the biblical writers that grab your heart. Then as you feel moved, write or sing some of your own psalms of love and praise to God.

4. Set a timer or use a "Pause App" to remind you to stop and say "I love You" to your Lord Jesus, the Lover of your Soul.

20. A Breakfast Story: Receiving the Serving Christ

Truly, truly, I say to you,
he who receives whomever I send receives Me…
John 13: 20 NASB

Are you more of a giver than a receiver? Maybe you don't want to "put anyone out." Maybe you feel pressured to "pay it back," if someone gives you a gift or does you a favor. I used to be that way until the Lord opened my eyes at a very difficult time in the life of our family.

1998 was a year of multiple health crises for our children. As I reflected on the months that preceded that difficult year, I remembered an incident I call, my "Breakfast Story." It was then the Lord taught me a lesson I would need during those crises just nine months later.

I was teaching through the Gospel of John in our ladies Bible study group. We came to the familiar passage in John, chapter 13, the story of Jesus washing the disciples' feet. That week I also had a breakfast date with a dear friend. Our usual breakfast place was a fun, "local-color" place called *Sam & Ethel's*.

So that lovely spring morning, I drove through the country roads on the way to her home. And I was listening to John 13 on a CD. All of a sudden, Christ's interaction with Peter grabbed my attention. Peter was boldly refusing to let Jesus wash his feet.

Watch what happens:

Jesus, knowing that the Father had given all things into His hands, and that He had come forth from God and was going back to God, got up from supper, and laid aside His garments; and taking a towel, He girded Himself.

Then He poured water into the basin, and began to wash the disciples' feet and to wipe them with the towel with which He was girded.

So He came to Simon Peter. He said to Him, "Lord, do You wash my feet?"

Jesus answered and said to him, "What I do you do not realize now, but you will understand hereafter."

Peter said to Him, "Never shall You wash my feet!"

Jesus answered him, "If I do not wash you, you have no part with Me."

Simon Peter said to Him, "Lord, then wash not only my feet, but also my hands and my head."

Jesus later replied, "… If I then, the Lord and the Teacher, washed your feet, you also ought to wash one another's feet. For I gave you an example that you also should do as I did to you."

Now here was the clincher for me...

"…Truly, truly, I say to you, he who receives whomever I send receives Me; and he who receives Me receives Him who sent Me."

Wait a minute...if I don't wash you, you have no part with Me...whomever I send receives Me...and Him who sent Me.

The Holy Spirit began to speak to my heart,

"Jan, you not only need to wash your bothers' and sisters' feet, but you also need to graciously let them wash your feet. Otherwise, you may be missing what I want to do for you through them."

It hit me so hard, I had to pull over and write down what the Lord was saying to me. It was a lesson I needed. I had a tendency to always be doing the giving. Maybe it was because I am a leader. Maybe it's my type A personality. Maybe it's pride. It was hard for me to be on the receiving end. But the Lord was telling me to "let my feet be washed" and graciously receive it as Him.

So I got back on the road and continued driving. I picked up my friend and arrived at *Sam & Ethel*'s. As we sat in that quaint country restaurant and opened our menus, my friend said to me,

"Today, I'm paying the bill."

Now I have to tell you that this precious sister does not have much extra cash. I was ready to protest, when the Lord spoke to my heart,

"Don't be like Peter. Receive this as a gift from Me. Let her wash your feet."

And so I did.

And this wonderful experience of the Serving Christ through my precious sister in the Lord, that spring day, prepared me to receive in our time of suffering, just nine months later. I was able to receive Christ's washing—meals, notes, scriptures, advice (yes, even unsolicited advice), house cleaning, the presence of "strangers," and of course, prayer, prayer, and more prayer.

So dear brothers and sisters, siblings in the family of God, could you be missing out on Christ ministering to you? He may want to meet your specific need through a brother or sister. Humbly receive and "let your feet be washed. "

Do you have a tendency to always do "pay back" when someone gives to you? Or can you receive and leave it there? Remember, when you graciously receive, you are giving to the giver the gift of joyful gratitude.

On the other side, has the Lord been moving you to wash someone's feet in a specific way? Maybe you've been holding back, thinking it's not a big deal. It is a big deal. Jesus wants to serve your brother or sister through you. Present yourself to Him as His instrument. We are His hands and feet.

Receiving and Serving Christ
At times the Lord calls us to generously give
Sometimes to graciously receive.

We are the hands and feet of our God
All of us who believe.

Let's not hold back blessings
We may be possessing

That are meant for someone nearby.
Let blessings flow through us

For He will renew us
With His favor from on high.

Also let others bless you
Let their kindness caress you

And be thankful for what they do.
For when you accept and are grateful

To one of the faithful
You will be blessing them too.
              Penny Mandeville

<u>Prayer</u>

Jesus, what an honor to be your hands, your feet, your arms, your voice, your people as You serve others through us. And open our eyes to see You, as our brothers and sisters are caring for us in Your Name. Teach us to graciously receive and "gift the giver" with our gratitude. In Your Name. Amen.

<u>Reflections</u>

1. In your journal, make a list of everything you have received this

week through the graciousness of another. Do you feel the need to do "pay back"?

2. Thank God for those who gave to you and recognize the Lord graciously serving you through them. Resist the urge to do "pay back."

3. Find this song on YouTube and enjoy being the expresser of God's life in your world.

We are His hands
We are His feet
We are His people
Children of the Lord[26]
Whiteheart

21. The Dance Partner: Yielding to His Lead

You have turned my mourning into joyful dancing
…and clothed me with joy.
Psalm 30:11 NLT

During a gathering with friends several years ago, I shocked them with my answer to an "icebreaker" question.

If you could do anything other than what you currently do, what would that be?
What is your secret ambition?

To everyone's surprise (including my husband's), my answer was "be a dancer." A dancer?

Why, dancer? I think it must be the grace, the ease of movement, the freedom. I'm always jealous when I watch dancers moving so effortlessly across the floor to the rhythm of the music.

I remember when I was a child how my dad taught us girls to dance the fox trot. The ballroom dances were nothing to that WWII generation of men. So our dad whisked my sisters and me, one by one, around the "ballroom" (our living room) with strength and grace.

My husband is not a "dancer" in any way, shape, or form. So dancing hasn't been a part of my adult life—except for short spurts of "dance parties" with baby grandsons or polkas with my mom and sisters.

But in preparation for our son's wedding, John and I signed up for dance lessons. The problem was I ended up taking the lead more often than not. And the few times I danced at family weddings with my brother Conrad, it usually started out as a tug of war. But when I surrendered to his lead, he would whisk me around the floor effortlessly.

I can't help but think of my life in union with Christ as a dance. I have the Perfect Dance Partner dwelling within. He has perfect rhythm. He has a strong hold on me and knows all the steps. And He can actually execute them.

I often try to lead to get Him to go my way. But when I yield to Him moment by moment, day by day, we dance together. He whisks me along in the way of His Spirit as the unique, gifted, "charming" person that He has created me to be.

As I yield to His life-giving flow, I experience

- skill beyond my skill,
- love beyond my love,
- words beyond my words,
- forgiveness beyond my forgiveness,
- fullness beyond my fullness.

What about you, my dear friend? Are you experiencing the life of Christ in and through you as you? Or do you continue to struggle to take the lead? Why not relinquish your will to His Almighty Self? Experience the effortless movement of the dance of faith—life in the Spirit.

<u>The Dance</u>
It's time to surrender
It's time to rejoice
It's time to be thankful
That I am your choice.

I trust where you'll lead me
As you reach out your hand.
Knowing where we're going
Is Your divine plan.
    Penny Mandeville

<u>Prayer</u>
O Loving Jesus, Indwelling Lord, teach me to not resist Your lead but to rather yield myself to You, as we dance together through every situation of my life, especially this one <u>(name what you are going through</u>). In Your Almighty Name. Amen.

<u>Reflections</u>
1. Put on some of your favorite praise music. Find a place with room to move. And move to the music in the arms of the Lover of your soul. Feel yourself yielding to him. Then ask yourself,

- Am I being whisked along in the way of the Spirit or am I trying to take the lead?
- How can I yield to the Lord today in the circumstances that I find myself?
- Journal your thoughts and prayers.

2. This dance is not just about Jesus and us. We believers, children of God, have been invited into the divine dance of the Trinity.

Our early church Fathers of the faith understood the mystery of the Trinity, not in a static way, as we modern Christians tend to do. Rather they saw it in an active way, as a dance. And they had a beautifully descriptive term for this Divine Trinitarian Dance: *perichoresis.*

> If you spell out the…Greek word, peri-choresis, you can hear in English what the word conveys: "peri" (from which we get words such as "perimeter") and "choresis" (from which we get our word "choreography") — a dancing circle. The word describes the interrelationships of the persons of the Trinity. That in everything God the Trinity is and does, each of the persons relates to and engages with each of the other persons. Like an eternal dance, the "choreography" of the Divine Being is singular in its diversity and diverse in its unity. And for church fathers, one beautiful way of understanding our salvation is our being invited into this dance.[27]
> Rankin Wilbourne, *Union with Christ*

Many others throughout church history have echoed the theme of union and communion with God as the heart of being a Christian. Participation in the divine dance of the Trinity is God's amazing invitation to us.

> The whole dance, or drama, or pattern of this three-Personal life is to be played out in each one of us: or (putting it the other way round) each one of us has got to enter that pattern, take his place in the dance. There is no other way to the

happiness for which we were made…Once a man is united to God, how could he not live forever?... But how is he to be united to God? How is it possible for us to be taken into the three-Personal life?… Now the whole offer which Christianity makes is this: that we can, if we let God have His way, come to share in the life of Christ…The whole purpose of becoming a Christian is simply nothing else."[28] C.S. Lewis, *Mere Christianity*

Think about that…deeply. Amen.

22. Social Anxiety: Really Seeing People

Don't be selfish; don't try to impress others.
Be humble, thinking of others as better than yourselves.
Don't look out only for your own interests,
but take an interest in others, too.
Philippians 2:3-4 NLT

Birthdays, holidays, special occasions, kids' school programs, neighborhood open houses, family gatherings, office parties, and more -- all are reasons for social occasions. And for many of us, anxiety ensues.

Add to the occasions themselves, questions like, "What do I wear? What do the kids wear?" And if we are hosting, add in preparations of cleaning, decorating, cooking, along with shopping and wrapping. It can all send us over the edge.

Hold on. Let's take a breath and look at what can help tremendously with "social anxiety."

When I was raising a young family, I used to listen religiously to Christian radio. One day, a speaker was exploring the topic of social anxiety. What the speaker said that day has stayed with me all these years. And when I keep these simple truths in mind as I enter a social situation, everything changes in my mind and heart. I get perspective – God's perspective. When I don't, it can all crash and burn really fast.

The speaker shared that many of us, when entering a social situation, have the attitude,

"Here I am. Pay attention to me. Ask about me."

Or I might add, if an introvert, we may be thinking,

> "Here I am. Don't pay attention to me. Don't ask about me. Let me hide somewhere or just listen."

Notice where the focus is—on me, either way. Rather, better to enter a social situation, saying,

> "There YOU are. Let me pay attention to YOU. Let me ask about YOU."

Brennan Manning says it this way,

> "Craving the approbation withheld in childhood, my false self staggers into each day with an insatiable appetite for affirmation. With my cardboard façade intact, I enter a roomful of people preceded by a muted trumpet -- "Here I am" -- whereas my true self hidden with Christ in God cries, "Oh, there you are!"[29]

Why not try this the next time you are with people? Ask the Holy Spirit to remind you to shift the focus off yourself onto the person with you.

I think Jesus lived that way, always present to people right there before Him. The religious leaders didn't really see people. They never "saw" the handicapped, the mentally ill, the sick, the outcasts, the un-religious, the "sinners." Jesus saw these "invisible people."

Who is "invisible" to you and your "crowd" today? If you are young, maybe it's older people. If you are healthy and strong, maybe it's the weak and sickly. You get the idea. Next time, why not "say" to one of those people who are usually "invisible" to you, "There you are. Let me pay attention to you. Let me ask about you."

Maybe, just maybe, you and I can be Christ's instruments to reach out to those around us. After all, He is the indwelling, loving Christ -- the greatest Gift to share with those we encounter each day.

<u>Your Instrument</u>
When I'm in a crowded room
Let me not despair.
May I think not of myself
But of others who are there.

Perhaps there's someone suffering
From a burden they can't bear.
Or someone maybe needs a friend
Or another may want prayer.

May I be your instrument
To encourage them to share.
Give me Your Holy Boldness
To show them that You care.
       Penny Mandeville

<u>Prayer</u>
Lord, make me an instrument of thy peace.
Where there is hatred, let me sow love;
Where there is injury, pardon;
Where there is doubt, faith;

Where there is despair, hope;
Where there is darkness, light;
Where there is sadness, joy.
O divine Master, grant that I may not so much seek
To be consoled as to console,
To be understood as to understand,
To be loved as to love;
For it is in giving that we receive;
It is in pardoning that we are pardoned;
It is in dying that we are born to eternal life.
        Prayer of St Francis

<u>Reflections</u>
As you go through your day, ask your indwelling Lord, to open your eyes to see those around you – the invisible ones and the obnoxious ones and everyone in between. Focus on them – see them, ask them, smile, appropriately touch. Make your encounter about them and not about you, in Jesus' Name.

23. The Misfit: Belonging Anywhere

So let us go out to him, outside the camp,
and bear the disgrace he bore.
Hebrews 13: 13 NLT

Have you ever felt like a misfit? Like you don't belong? Welcome to the club. Actually, feeling out of place can be a good thing. Let me explain.

Our church small group met to conclude our year-long study in the important letter to the Hebrews. Memories flooded my mind as we discussed one of the concluding exhortations found in chapter 13.

> *. . . Jesus suffered and died outside the city gates to make his people holy by means of his own blood. So <u>let us go out to him, outside the camp, and bear the disgrace he bore.</u> For this world is not our permanent home; we are looking forward to a home yet to come.* Hebrews 13:12-14 NLT (emphasis added)

I have often felt "outside the camp" even among the different Christian groups (or "camps") with whom we have been associated over the years. Somehow it seemed that there was a certain "persona" that was characteristic of the group. And the in-crowd all acted the same way, emphasized the same "truths," used the same vocabulary, and often even looked like one another.

I would feel the subtle pressure to think and believe and, at times, even look the same way to fit in. But it didn't work for me for long. What had started out to be a good time of growing together, for me, often deteriorated into a rebellion of sorts. I would feel like I needed to sell my soul to the group image to really fit in. And I couldn't do that. God had been working dramatically in my life to free me of "Christian conformity" – following a particular group's list of do's & don'ts. And it seemed that each group had its own list.

So finally, I came to the point of crying out to God,

> "LORD, I don't fit anywhere."

Then came His quiet reply,

> "You don't fit anywhere, so you can fit anywhere." [read that again slowly]

The Holy Spirit's words set my soul free. I no longer felt a need "to fit" anywhere. So I could go into a group and just be who God made me to be. I could let Jesus live His loving and serving life in and through me, as me, no matter where I was. I could take my cues from Him because He is the owner of my life.

How about you, dear brother and sister? Do you feel like you don't fit anywhere? Great news. You can fit anywhere because you don't fit anywhere. Don't let any group or individual define you.

No one owns you, except the Lover of your Soul. Let Him live and love and serve through you no matter where you are.

<u>My Temporary Home</u>
Lord, I don't belong here.
There's no one just like me.

I'm different from the ones I know
From friends or family.

Perhaps because I'm in this world
Only temporarily.

My true home is with You,
My Lord, for all eternity.

There I'll join with all the Saints
Who have come home before me.

And my soul no longer longing
Will finally be set free.

Till then I will just be
Who You created me to be.
Penny Mandeville

<u>Prayer</u>

Dear Lover of my soul, my Father God with Whom I always "fit." What freedom when I remember I belong to You alone. I can go anywhere You call me, because You live, love, and serve through me. I can be me, and I can accept others as they are, no matter whether I am accepted or not. I am accepted by You in Your Beloved Son. In Jesus' Name. Amen.

<u>Reflections</u>

1. Ask the Lord to show you the different "masks" you have worn over the years in order to fit into the various groups you have been a part of or tried to be. Confess your self-rejection and thank Him for His forgiveness.

2. Reflect on this truth,

> *Living from the heart Jesus gave you means being the person you were designed to be, acting like yourself in all situations.*[30]

Can you act like yourself in all situations? Meditate on:

> *But by the grace of God I am what I am, and his grace toward me was not in vain. On the contrary, I worked harder than any of them, though it was not I, but the grace of God that is with me.* 1 Corinthians 15:10 ESV

3. Ask God to reveal to you who you really are and begin listing the thoughts that come. Then ask Him to empower you to be who you truly are in every situation you face.

GLORY IN THE EVERYDAY

Nothing is too great for His almighty Power.
Nothing is too small for His Love.[31]
Corrie ten Boom
Tramp for the Lord

24. Salt Deficit: Flavoring His World

But what good is salt if it has lost its flavor?
Can you make it salty again?
It will be thrown out and trampled underfoot as worthless.
Matthew 5:13 NLT

Salt. What a prolific commodity. In the past salt was valuable and rare. But now it is cheap, always there, on the table, in the cupboard. Available. And so taken for granted -- by me, at least, until one day…

All of a sudden, my little known (and barely paid attention to) condition known as *hyponatremia* (low sodium blood levels) came crashing in with extreme confusion, fatigue, irritability, etc. Circumstances and neglect on my part had created the "perfect storm." It was scary. But surprisingly all was well after ingesting a glass of water containing...you guessed it, SALT. Humble, vital, but easily forgotten, salt.

So this has gotten me thinking about common table salt.

Jesus used salt as a metaphor for us children of God. But what is it about salt that prompted Jesus to say to us, "You are the *salt* of the earth?"

Notice Jesus didn't say, "You can be the salt of the earth" or "You should be the salt of the earth." He said, "You are the salt of the earth." So somehow my identity as a believer is wrapped up with the picture of salt? Why salt?

Salt is a necessity of life and was a mineral that was used since ancient times in many cultures a seasoning, a preservative, a disinfectant, a component of ceremonial offerings, and as a unit of exchange. In various contexts, it is used metaphorically to signify permanence, loyalty, durability, fidelity, usefulness, value, and purification. (Wikipedia, *Salt in the Bible*).[32]

Today salt is still used to enhance flavors and, as I found out painfully, to maintain good health by providing biochemical balance. Salt is pretty amazing.

And so is a child of God.

Our just being "who we are in Who He Is" can change our world -- not because of us, but because of Who lives in us and through us as us.

The New Testament contains two passages that help us see and savor our *saltiness* as followers of our Lord.

Salt is good for seasoning. But if it loses its flavor, how do you make it salty again? You must have the qualities of salt among yourselves and live in peace with each other.
Mark 9:50 NLT

Walk in wisdom toward outsiders, making the best use of the time. Let your speech always be gracious, seasoned with salt, so that you may know how you ought to answer each person.
Colossians 4:5-6 ESV

My Vietnamese friend Tuyet, now with Jesus, was a "salty sister in the Lord." At Tuyet's memorial service, a friend of hers named Lee told about how she had met Tuyet. Lee ran a grocery store in Tuyet's neighborhood. Lee had delivered a baby just days before they met, but she had no interest in him. Lee was on the brink of suicide, despairing of life.

Meanwhile, Tuyet had a strange prompting. She had no money and wasn't in the market for anything in particular. But Tuyet was impelled to go to Lee's store. Once in that store, Tuyet told Lee about her prompting. It was then Lee spilled out her anguish and despair and disinterest in her baby. The long and short of it is Tuyet came alongside Lee in the depths of her misery. And she was able to share the love of God with Lee. Lee became thirsty for Tuyet's Jesus because of the *salt of the earth* resident in one little humble child of God from Vietnam.

Lee started caring for her baby. Tuyet and Lee began reading the Scriptures together day by day, and the little group of two humble believers were joined by another, then another, then still others. And they all continued to read the Scriptures together day by day. The *salt of the earth* preserved a life and caused that life to be thirsty for Life indeed.

<u>Preserver of My Soul</u>
You purify my heart
You restore my soul
You renew my spirit
You make me whole.

You preserve my life
And make it yours

So out of my heart
Your love pours

You season Your Word
With Your Holy Spirit
It changes the lives
Of those who hear it.
        Penny Mandeville

<u>Prayer</u>
Oh Jesus, what an amazing honor to be the salt of the earth. What an identity, what a calling—to be Your preserver, your seasoning, your thirst-producer in a desperate, rotting world.
Oh, be that in and through me today. In Your glorious, thirst-quenching Name. Amen.

<u>Reflections</u>
1. In your journal, write out the verses quoted in the devotional. Ask the Lord to speak to you by His Spirit.

2. Ask Him who in your life needs a sprinkle of "Jesus through you." Follow His promptings as He opens the way.

3. Journal your thoughts and prayers.

25. My Mother-in-Law's Sifter: Letting Go

Therefore we do not lose heart.
Though outwardly we are wasting away,
yet inwardly we are being renewed day by day.
2 Corinthians 4:16 NIV

It was many years ago now...the day we boxed up the items my mother-in-law was discarding. She was needing to downsize. Betty Jean Loyd was moving to a senior community, states away from where she had lived most of her adult life. Far from where she had married a man and raised an only son.

At 80 years of age, Betty Jean, an only child, knew that she needed to be near us, her only family. So we helped her box up her no-longer-needed things.

And there it was—her sifter.

No. Not her sifter.

Betty had used that sifter day after day, month after month, year after year to do the delicious baking and cooking she was known for. Along with her amazing flower garden, needlework and sewing, my MIL cooked and baked. Delicious food, lovely cakes and desserts.

It overwhelmed me, deeply. I can't explain it. For a long time, I cried thinking of that stage of her life done for good. Those days of cooking and cleaning and caring for a little family. Now the disassembling of a life. The ending of a beloved stage of life. The pending "good-bye" that certainly was closer than ever. The brevity of life. All of that and more spoke to me in her sifter.

As the days and years have unfolded, that well-used and loved sifter began to say something more. It spoke of what happens to all of us as we live on this broken, fallen earth. Our lives get sifted, slowly eliminating the earthly, superficial stuff of what our human lives consist -- our possessions, our abilities, our energies, even our understanding and awareness.

We fight the sifting, the stripping, the emptying; instead of embracing our reality today, each day. But wise are we when we walk through each "valley of the shadow" with the Shepherd and Guardian of our Souls. We can trust Him to put it all together to fulfill His purpose in and through our lives. What will remain after the sifting are the eternal, enduring treasures of life indeed.

So we can declare with the psalmist David,

> The Lord is my shepherd;
>   I have all that I need.
> 2 He lets me rest in green meadows;
>   he leads me beside peaceful streams.
> 3 He renews my strength.
> He guides me along right paths,
>   bringing honor to his name.
> 4 Even when I walk
>   through the darkest valley,
> I will not be afraid,
>   for you are close beside me.
> Your rod and your staff
>   protect and comfort me.

[5] You prepare a feast for me
    in the presence of my enemies.
  You honor me by anointing my head with oil.
    My cup overflows with blessings.
[6] Surely your goodness and unfailing love will pursue me
    all the days of my life,
    and I will live in the house of the Lord
    forever.   Psalm 23 NLT

P.S. Betty Jean Loyd passed into eternity on Wednesday, November 23, 2016 at 9:15pm. Betty's *sifting* has ended. So now she has no need of the stuff that she shed in this life. Betty Jean is finally home.

Things
We accumulate the tools we need
Down through the ages.
But the things we use often change
Along with life's stages.

What once was a necessity
Now just takes up space.
So we put it in the donate bag
And something useful takes its place.

Some things come and some things go.
But somethings we hold dear.
Like photographs of loved ones
Remain year after year.

But even these we'll leave behind
When we finally depart

When He calls us home
What we'll bring alone
Is the love within our hearts
          Penny Mandeville

<u>Prayer</u>
Lord, how I cling to this life and all the "stuff" that seems so important, so necessary. And how I hate the sifting, the stripping of all I call mine (which isn't mine, really). Give me Your perspective on what life on this earth is all about. And open my eyes to see You as my true Source in life and in death. In my Shepherd's strong and tender Name. Amen.

<u>Reflections</u>
1. Do you feel yourself being sifted in any way? Talk to the Lord about it, making note of it in your journal.

2. Then write out Psalm 23 and observe how your Good Shepherd meets your needs, even right now. Start making a list, thanking Him for His provision even in the midst of the sifting.

3. Maybe it's time to voluntarily begin letting go of things you have kept too long. Pass them on to others who can use and enjoy them. If there are too many memories connected to an item, consider keeping just a part (such as one dish or a cup and saucer from a set of dishes). Pass the rest on. As Richard Rohr (*Everything Belongs*) says, "All great spirituality is about letting go."[33] So maybe let's start with a few material things.

26. The Cupcake: Being Loved in the "Little"

And may you have the power to understand…
how wide, how long, how high, and how deep his love is.
May you experience the love of Christ,
though it is too great to understand fully.
Ephesians 3:20 NLT

Have you ever assumed that God is too busy to be concerned about the small things in your life? After all, He has the entire universe and the world of people's huge problems to attend to. Well, years ago while a student at Moody Bible Institute, I learned otherwise. God tenderly cared for us in so many "little ways," as well as big. And it was during those student days that I came across a quote that I have never forgotten:

Nothing is too great for His almighty Power.
Nothing is too small for His Love.[26]
Corrie ten Boom

Through the years God's love has held true – in both the big and the small. But recently, God totally knocked my socks off. He proved once again that nothing is too "small" in my life for Him to show His love for me.

This is what was going on. I was preparing for our daughter in-law Cortney's birthday gift. We already had an awesome card. A large, beautifully decorated cupcake filled the cover, surrounded by the words:

You are a beautiful cupcake in a world of muffins.

Then the simple message on the inside:

HAPPY BIRTHDAY

It was such a perfect card for several reasons:

- Cortney is beautiful (like the cupcake), but needs gluten free baked goods to keep her health on keel.

- Cortney is surrounded by males in her home — Jeremy her husband, Evan & Carter her sons, and even 2 male dogs (ok, and one female dog but she doesn't count in this illustration).

- I'm known for my muffins and often do a muffin drop at their home for our two grandsons.

The quirky idea I had was to replicate the imagery of the card with a big beautiful gluten free cupcake in the middle of a tray and surround the gf cupcake (a.k.a. Cortney) with muffins of various types to represent her boys — chocolate chip (Carter's favorite); pumpkin chocolate chip (Evan's favorite); lemon (Jeremy's favorite and Carter's 2nd favorite).

A couple days before the birthday dinner, we went to find *The Neighborhood Nest,* a gluten free bakery in a neighboring town. Oh, the gf cupcakes were beautiful and yummy — chocolate (of course), vanilla raspberry, and cherry chip. I couldn't decide. The only problem was…they were small. So I bought all three. Then on to *Hobby Lobby* to find a tray and wrapping paper.

As I made my way up and down aisles in *Hobby Lobby*, I was grieving about the smallness of Cortney's gf cupcakes.

I thought, "One small cupcake will look dwarfed in the midst of the muffins. But I suppose I could put all three on the tray. Even though that isn't really the imagery of the card, it will have to do."

I resigned myself to doing the best I could with the cupcakes and tray.

But just then I turned the corner into the next aisle. And what I saw froze me dead in my tracks–there in the middle of the aisle

…on the floor

…was a huge, gorgeously decorated

… CUPCAKE.

Yes, cupcake!

Not an edible cupcake, but one in the shape of a small sparkly pink "hatbox" with a topping of "luscious white icing-like fluffy stuff" poofing up from the top.

Right there, on the floor, in the middle of the aisle.

No joke!

I was dumbfounded…speechless…awestruck!

At first, I didn't move…what? where? who?

I looked around. It didn't seem to have fallen off of a nearby shelf. No kids were nearby, no moms, no one.

When I finally "came to," I slowly rolled my cart toward the "cupcake." I hesitatingly picked it up, turned it over, and guess what it said.

"Cupcake Box"

CUPCAKE BOX!

I opened it and realized the three small gluten free cupcakes would fit perfectly in that beautifully decorated, just the right size, CUPCAKE BOX.

What ecstasy. What delight.

O Jesus, You are too funny! You are too awesome!

As I continued my shopping, I felt ten feet off the ground with pure joy.

Then I turned another corner and saw the perfect pink tray for the perfect Cupcake Box. So I put the box in the middle with the muffins all around.

And on the big day, it was double delight to bring Cortney her beautiful present with its meaningful card. And then I told her the amazing story of how God shopped with us that day at *Hobby Lobby*.

Now all glory to God, who is able, through his mighty power at work within us, to accomplish infinitely more than we might ask or think.
Ephesians 3:20 NLT

Each Moment
Jesus loves to join us
In the tasks we have at hand.

He loves when we acknowledge Him
In everything we plan.

He's present in each moment
Whether mundane or quite grand.

How blessed I am to know how much
He cares and understands.
Penny Mandeville

Prayer
O Jesus, You are too funny. You are too awesome. You are too loving — over the top. Truly, nothing is too small. And I didn't even ask. I just thought. But I couldn't have imagined how You would love me so perfectly that day. And how You would love dear Cortney. She was able to see the metaphor of the card and her glorious life with her wonderful men all around her.
All glory to You, O God…even before we ask or think. Over and above. Great or small. Amen.

Reflections
1. What little things has God done for you? Have you just assumed they were coincidence?

2. Ask the Holy Spirit to bring to your remembrance His "little loving things" that you may have never noticed. And thank Him today.

27. The Nightgown: Living from the New

…you stripped off the old self with its evil practices,
and have put on the new self,
which is being renewed to a true knowledge
according to the image of the One who created it.
Colossians 3:9-10 NASB

About 20 years ago, I bought a beautiful nightgown to keep me warm and feminine in the cold Ohio winters. I've loved that nightgown. I could wrap myself in it and be cozy and comfortable.   And despite the fact that it's faded and worn, I've had a hard time giving it up to the ragbag. Every year as the weather has turned colder, I've taken it out of the rag bag to put it on "just one more year."

Now my husband is not a rich man, but he is a good provider. He has enabled me to have other beautiful options. But they are not as comfortable to my "flesh" as that old "friend."

Yet in reality, that old rag is not consistent with who I am as John's wife –a well-loved and cared for woman. I just have a hard time putting on those new gowns. So out "she" comes for yet another season.

It's the same way with our spiritual clothing as beloved believers united to our True Lover Jesus Christ. He has provided His own beautiful character as clothing for our human life on this earth: love, forgiveness, kindness, truth, compassion, peace, self-control.

But what do we do? We continually go back into the "ragbag" of our fleshly life before Christ. We put on those comfortable

characteristics that are inconsistent with who we are in
Christ: things such as jealousy & competition, unforgiveness,
sexual immorality & impurity, pride, greed, and the like.

God says to put those off. Every time we are tempted to live out of
the ragbag, we can chose to "put on the Lord Jesus Christ and make
no provision for the flesh to gratify its desires."
 Romans 13:14 ESV

After all, the indwelling Lord Jesus Christ is our wardrobe. He
Himself is our Life. We are united with Him in His fullness. So we
reckon to be true what really is true – we are holy, righteous, and
redeemed in Him. By choosing Christ in all His fulness of character,
we are at the same time laying aside the ragbag characteristics of our
flesh apart from Christ.

> Your old life is dead. Your new life, which is your real
> life…is with Christ in God. He is your life…Now you're
> dressed in a new wardrobe. Every item of your new way of
> life is custom-made by the Creator, with his label on it. All the
> old fashions are now obsolete.

> So, chosen by God for this new life of love, dress in the
> wardrobe God picked out for you: compassion, kindness,
> humility, quiet strength, discipline. Be even-tempered, content
> with second place, quick to forgive an offense. Forgive as
> quickly and completely as the Master forgave you. And
> regardless of what else you put on, wear love. It's your basic,
> all-purpose garment. Never be without it.
> Colossians 3:3-14 MSG

<u>Freedom in Him</u>
When the Lord shows us freedom
From our fleshly ways
Why would we ever return
To those days?

A butterfly who's finally
Left its cocoon
Would never go back
To confinement and gloom.

Why would we choose
What bound us up tight
And made us miserable
And ready to fight?

So let's rest in His wisdom
His strength and His peace.
For His patience, forgiveness
And love never cease.
          Penny Mandeville

<u>Prayer</u>
Father, thank you for the exquisite Life You have given me in Your Son. I am in Him and He is in me. Show me how to experience the beauty of Your New Life. Teach me to put on Your perfect "clothing" every day as I go out into my "today." In Jesus' Name. Amen.

<u>Reflections</u>
1. For further meditation, spend some time in this passage.

My old self has been crucified with Christ. It is no longer I who live, but Christ lives in me. So I live in this earthly body by trusting in the Son of God, who loved me and gave himself for me.   Galatians 2:20 ESV

Pete Briscoe summarizes Galatians 2:20
I died. I'm indwelt. I'm depending[34]

2. Journal what the Holy Spirit "highlights" to your mind and heart.

28. The Pantry: Storing His Words for Your Soul

... receive with meekness the implanted word,
which is able to save your souls.
James 1:21b ESV

Are you in the midst of a long stretch of days, maybe even months, when you feel like you have nothing? Maybe you are a mother of multiple preschoolers; a person in chronic pain; a cancer patient going through chemo; a husband or wife, a son or daughter, a sister or brother grieving the sudden death of your loved one; or maybe a caregiver of some kind. It has been survival day after day. You don't have enough time or energy or mental clarity to replenish your own resources. And yet, somehow you are making it, if only barely.

Well, I get it. Several years ago, we were helping our daughter and son-in-law and young family do a military move. This move had multiple twists and turns along the way. I felt empty, totally depleted energy-wise. But in the midst of the fray, God was my sufficiency. I made it, despite how tiring and constant and "walking on the edge" it was. I remembered that there is a storehouse, a pantry that is Him and yes, His indwelling Word—the sacred words that have been engrafted into my soul over the years.

> He said to them, "Therefore every scribe who has become
> a disciple of the kingdom of heaven is like a head of a
> household, who brings forth out of his treasure [storehouse,
> pantry] things new and old" Matthew 13:52 NASB
> (emphasis added).

The *scribes* were teachers, experts in Scripture truth. They may or may not have had a personal relationship with the God about whom they taught. But in this verse, Jesus says if a person knows the Scriptures as they did AND becomes His *disciple,* that person will have a *storehouse* from which to draw. That person will receive new truth in addition to known (old) truth—*whatever is needed at the time.* And it's all because of relationship with Him who is the Truth.

It's like my kitchen cabinet filled with pottery, both old and new. Because I have that storehouse/ reservoir of pottery, I can go there and pull out some of my new Polish pottery and arrange it on the table to make a beautiful setting with an old blue and white pitcher.

What about YOU, dear child of God? What is the storehouse, the pantry, YOU are drawing from? Is it the Living God revealed in His engrafted Word stored in your inner person?

When you hit those dark, dry, depleted times, trust the indwelling Holy Spirit. He will take the implanted, engrafted Word and feed you. He loves and cares for you!

And in your times of relative calm, why not spend more time in the Scriptures? Even sign up for a small group Bible study. Join a group of sisters or brothers and study the Word together.

Grab hold of your Resource for whatever you may be going through. He is sufficient for every need. Open the pantry of His Word and feed on truth for your soul. And then when times are hard and life is intense, the "engrafted word" in the power of the indwelling Spirit will "rescue your soul."

> ...God's mystery, which is Christ, in whom are hidden all the
> treasures of wisdom and knowledge....For in him the

whole fullness of deity dwells bodily, and you have been filled in him... Colossians 2:2b-3,9-10 ESV

All Scripture is breathed out by God and profitable for teaching, for reproof, for correction, and for training in righteousness, that the man of God may be complete, equipped for every good work. 2Timothy 3:16-17 ESV

Abide in me, and I in you. As the branch cannot bear fruit by itself, unless it abides in the vine, neither can you, unless you abide in me. I am the vine; you are the branches. Whoever abides in me and I in him, he it is that bears much fruit, for apart from me you can do nothing....If you abide in me, and my words abide in you, ask whatever you wish, and it will be done for you.   John 15:4-5,7 ESV

His Word

His word is a reservoir
It's all I'll ever need.
The wisdom from my Jesus
His teachings set me free.

His word holds all the answers
To questions of this world.
Waiting to be discovered
Waiting to be unfurled.

So I go into my storehouse
Searching for His truth
Something He has just revealed
Or a nugget from my youth.
　　　Penny Mandeville

<u>Prayer</u>

Lord Jesus, Author of Your beautiful Words, bury those precious truths deep into my soul. So that when the hard times come, and I hardly have time to think, much less read and pray, Your indwelling Spirit will bring forth the engrafted Word to my mind and heart to save me. In Your faithful Name. Amen.

<u>Reflections</u>

1. What are some of your favorite Scripture verses or passages? Why are they your favorites? Write these out in your journal along with how God may have used them in your past.

2. Are there some verses that have been jumping out at you recently, maybe new ones that you never "noticed" before. Is there something going on in your life that the Holy Spirit may be speaking into? Note those as well.

3. Thank Him for His words, both "old and new," that feed your soul.

> Your words were found, and I ate them,
> And Your word was to me the joy and rejoicing of my heart;
> For I am called by Your name, O LORD God of hosts.
> Jeremiah 15:16 NKJV

GLORY IN FAMILY

*In every encounter we either give life
or we drain it.
There is no neutral exchange.
We either enhance human dignity, or we drain it.*[35]
Brennan Manning,
Abba's Child

29. We are FA-MI-LY: Loving Our Differences

See what great love the Father has lavished on us,
that we should be called children of God.
And that is what we are.
1 John 3:1 NASB

"We are fa-mi-ly...my mother, brothers, sisters, and me …"

OK, I did change the lyrics a bit. But that's who we Renners were after our dad died and before our mom went home to God. And I am blessed beyond measure to be a part of it all -- the oldest of seven (three girls and 4 boys). And the "Boss of the Mob" according to my mom.

So many families are a mess today. We're "a mess" too, but with one big difference. A rarity, in fact. We love and support one another. And we actually want to be together. What an undeserved gift, and I certainly know it.

Now don't get me wrong. Some of us are quite "crusty" -- a tad bit difficult to get along with. Then there are the "mushy-gushies"—the affectionate mercy-showers. And everything in between. And now with kids and grandkids entering the group, it can get kind of crazy. But it's crazy-good.

But above, around, over, and under it all is a lot of love and grace. Our Mom had always been our *cosmic glue*, so to speak. She said that when she's gone, we better get along and love each other. Otherwise, she would come back to haunt us. Ha, ha! And now she is gone to her home with Jesus. And I'm sure He is letting her know what a legacy of unconditional love she left us. We do get along, and more than that. We love being together.

Another thing about us Renners is that there are many others who are part of us, either permanently or temporarily. So over the years, the Renner family has included distant relatives, in-laws, out-laws, boyfriends and girlfriends, various friends, "enemies," pets, neighbors – *Renner-wanna-be's*, if you will. And that's a good thing. I grieve for others who don't have this closeness in their family (come be part of ours). I thank God for my human family. They are a gift.

But I realize that what we Renners have is just a feeble picture (as good as it is) of another family, a forever family -- God's family. Oh, on this earth, even God's children can be a bit crusty and hard to get along with. Or mushy-gushy mercy showers -- and everything in between. But no matter what, we belong to each other. We are united to each other in our Lord Jesus Christ, God's Son, our Brother and our true *Cosmic Glue.*

And He has gifted us uniquely to help and serve each other. These are called *grace* gifts because they are gifts from God. We can help and serve one another with His power and abilities. The Scriptures give us several lists (see Reflection #4). This is my favorite:

> God has given each of you a gift from his great variety of spiritual gifts. Use them well to serve one another. Do you have the gift of speaking? Then speak as though God himself were speaking through you. Do you have the gift of helping others? Do it with all the strength and energy that God supplies. Then everything you do will bring glory to God through Jesus Christ. 1 Peter 4:10-11 NLT

Let's thank God and love one another in the family of God. Let us appreciate the differences and giftings among us. And let's be on the look-out for those who are not yet in the family but may "wanna be."

Because *WE ARE FA-MI-LY*.   Truly.

<u>Family of God</u>
The family I belong to
Is spread around the earth.

We look so very different,
it's a family quite diverse.

We speak in different languages
And our customs aren't the same.

We have varied gifts and talents
But the thing we all proclaim

Is that Jesus is the Son of God
Our Savior and our Lord.

Despite our other differences
In this we're of one accord.
                Penny Mandeville

<u>Prayer</u>
Father of families, thank You for each and every one in my human family. What a gift you have given me to be part of one that isn't perfect, but in our own messy way has been loving and affirming. I pray for those who have only experienced pain and heartache in

their families. Heal them from the inside out, O tender Father. Cause them to cast their hurts and themselves on You, their only true Source of love and affirmation.

Open our eyes to our brothers and sisters all around. Move us to serve them in practical ways by Your Spirit. And teach us to graciously receive Your love and gifts flowing through them.

In Jesus, Your Son and our Brother. Amen.

Reflections

1. When you think of your human family or see a picture of one of them, thank God for that individual and what they have contributed to your life. If it was largely negative, entrust that person and yourself into the healing hands of your Abba Father God. Pray for them.

2. Next, think of your brothers and sisters in Christ. Thank God for the contribution each has made to your life. Note their differences from and their similarities to yourself. How has each of these enhanced your life?

3. As an optional Bible study, look up the following passages on spiritual gifts and list the gifts in your journal. Which gift/gifts do feel you have? Thank God and ask Him how you can serve others by exercising your gifts. Then ask God about those serving you in the family of God. Reach out and thank them for being instruments in God's hands to minister to you through their uniqueness.   (Romans 12: 6-8; 1 Corinthians 12:1-31; Ephesians 4:11-16; 1 Peter 4:10-11)

30. A Family Vacation: Becoming Like what We Focus On

But the fruit of the Spirit is love, joy …
Galatians 5:22 ESV

One year, when our kids were grown but not yet married and out of the nest, we had the most wonderful extended family reunion at Long Beach Island, New Jersey. Several of us siblings and families rented houses on the same block for the week. And we all (along with in-laws, friends, and pets) descended upon that little beach community.

It was a glorious week, filled with swimming, sunbathing, sunrise watching. But the best thing was the love and togetherness and community that just happened. We shared meals together, each family taking a turn. Some even joined my brother Conrad and me, official Sunrise Club members, in watching the sunrise. It was an amazing time of togetherness.

So a year or two later, some of us rented houses again at LBI. I was hoping to recapture the same experience of that previous vacation together. Well, you know how that goes. Recapturing glory usually never happens. And it certainly didn't happen that time. Or so I thought.

For one thing, we couldn't all make it for various valid reasons. On top of that, my brother Paul's family rented a house that was germ-infested. Every day other members of their family would drop like flies with a terrible flu-bug. So a skeleton crew from that household was on the beach.

We didn't eat together like the other year. There was little to no fellowship or community because of struggles going on in individual lives. So conversations were largely negative and depressing, rather than fun and light-hearted.

Not to bore you with too many negative details, let's just say that to me the vacation was a total bust! And I left Long Beach Island mad, mad, mad, and feeling cheated. For the 11-hour drive home from New Jersey to Ohio, I seethed. I couldn't sleep that night. And I stayed stuck for days, until . . .

The Lord broke through:

> Enough! Now it's over. Now, when you think of this vacation, I want you to come to me. Focus on the one hour of joyful bliss we had together.

Oh my goodness. I had forgotten about that glorious morning because of my absorption with my disappointment.

It was the Wednesday of vacation week. I woke up at 5:45 a.m. totally awake. Grabbing a large cup of coffee at Bageleddi's (the local favorite coffee/bagel shop), I walked alone to the beach. It was warm, pristine actually. The sun had just started to come up but was not yet visible. The cloudbank above the ocean was turning shades of pink, purple, and blue. Then the sliver of sun started to appear on the horizon. I opened my Bible and read in the Psalms:

> The heavens are telling of the glory of God;
> And their expanse is declaring the work of His hands . . .
> In them He has placed a tent for the sun.
> Which is like a bridegroom coming out of his chamber;
> It rejoices as a strong man to run his course.

Its rising is from one end of the heavens,
And its circuit to the other end of them;
And there is nothing hidden from its heat.
Psalm 19:1, 4–6 NASB

So Jesus and I walked and talked together that glorious morning—perfect rest in him. We enjoyed together the most gorgeous sunrise I had truly ever seen. And in my focus on all the negatives, I had forgotten it all.

 After the Lord's reminder, whenever negative thoughts about vacation would start to flood my mind, I remembered this one *joy*ful hour of bliss with my Lord. I aimed the thoughts of my mind and the affections of my heart toward the only One who deserves my total absorption.

As the days went by, something amazing started to happen. Other pleasant memories of our vacation started to surface—like my early morning walk to the beach, coming upon the delightful sight of my brothers and nephews fishing in the surf; and the fun supper at the Mud Hut with my husband and adult children; and an unexpected, deep conversation with a relative. By God's grace, he saved me from a root of bitterness in my heart.

As I began to reflect on what had happened in me, I started to realize what I've come to believe is a spiritual principle,

> *We become like what we focus on.*

I remembered this favorite passage of Scripture:

> But we all, with unveiled face, beholding as in a mirror the

glory of the Lord, are being transformed into the same image from glory to glory . . . For God, who said, "Light shall shine out of darkness," is the One who has shone in our hearts to give the Light of the knowledge of the glory of God in the face of Christ.   2 Corinthians 3:18; 4:6 NASB

What a transforming gaze. All because of His invitation,

Focus on me and remember joy.

Your Better Plan
Disappointment shades my thinking
Like a dark opaque screen.

I focus on what might have been
And miss what can be seen.

Help me hold my expectations
Loosely in my hand.

Ready to surrender to
Your far better plan.

I don't want to miss the chance
Of seeing what you do

So keep me always focused
Only on You.
> Penny Mandeville

Prayer
Lord, my expectations trip me up every time. Teach me through

your indwelling Spirit to continually turn my thoughts to You, because I really do become like what I focus on, don't I? Rescue me every time I'm distracted from You. Fill me with the joy of being transformed more and more into Your likeness while I'm living on this earth. Thank You. In Your Joy-filled, glorious Name. Amen.

<u>Reflections</u>

1. What's your attitude, your frame of mind, your *focus* right now? What is it that you set your mind on as you go through your day? Do you believe it's true that "we become like what we focus on"? Pray about your struggles, and get His perspective. Then journal your thoughts and prayers.

2. Check out these Scriptures. Even write them out in your journal. Pay attention to what the Holy Spirit "highlights" to your mind and heart.

     Colossians 3:1–4
     Philippians 4:8–9
     1 John 3:1–2
     Hebrews 12:1-3

3. As William Blake said, "They become what they behold."[36] What will you "behold" today? What or Who will you focus on?

31. Your Name: Being WOW-ed

God elevated him to the place of highest honor
and gave him the name above all other names,
that at the name of Jesus every knee should bow…
Philippians 2:9-10a NLT

"Tell us about your name…"

This was the ice-breaker at a teacher in-service I attended several years ago. I was glad for the topic, because I have an interesting name. In fact, each of my names is unique.

My full name is Janet Gale Renner Loyd. "Janet" is after my mother whose name is "Jeanette" (apparently my Polish grandfather had a French girlfriend during WWI by that name). My middle name, "Gale" is the first three letters of my mother's maiden name (Galuszka) G-A-L plus an E. My husband says that "Gale" is more appropriate than the usual "G-A-I-L," because of my similarity to a "whirlwind" (ha, ha). "Renner" is a German name and is a palindrome -- it can be spelled forward and backward the same way.

That leaves my married name, "Loyd." That's right, it IS spelled correctly. (I always spell it aloud, but people still insist on putting 2 L's). My flippant explanation for the one "L" spelling is "my husband had some lazy ancestors." And according to John's recent discoveries in *Ancestry*, this actually seems to be the case.

I wonder how Jesus would have answered the "ice breaker" question: "Tell us about your name."

He may have said, "My name 'Jesus' was given to my mother by an angel. It means 'Savior.' My title 'Christ' means 'Anointed One'—I am the Messiah, the Promised One foretold throughout generations."

He then might go on and on with significant name after significant name—names such as "Lord, King, the Lamb of God, the Alpha & Omega..."

But I suspect the reply He would most often give would be, "My name is 'I AM. I AM everything and anything you will ever need, because I AM Jehovah, God the Son."

Jesus wasn't hesitant to use this name to refer to Himself in His conversation with the religious leaders. He was almost stoned for blasphemy.

> Jesus said to them, "Truly, truly I say to you, before Abraham was born, I AM." So they picked up stones to throw at Him. John 8:58-59 NASB

This sacred name of God was not even allowed to be spoken by the devout Jew at that time, because it told of the very essence of God Himself -- the Eternal Present. His Essence is His Existence, LIFE itself.

Jesus further elaborated on this divine name in the rich metaphors of the Gospel of John.

> I AM the Bread of life. I AM the Light of the world. I AM the Door of the sheep. I AM the Good Shepherd. I AM the

Resurrection & the Life. I AM the Way, the Truth, & the Life. I AM the True Vine.
(See Gospel of John, chapters 6, 8, 10, 11, 14, 15)

Years ago, I found a treasure of a children's book called *God Says I AM: What God Tells Us About Himself in the Bible – from A to Z.*[37] This wonderful book goes through the whole alphabet describing who God is.

I challenged my five-year old grandson Kaden to learn all the descriptions of God in the *I AM* book. We practiced together whenever I visited. One of our times together was especially precious. After Kaden & I sat together seeing how much we could remember, I went back through, quickly repeating all of the descriptions.

God says **I AM** – the **A**rtist, the **B**uilder, the **C**reator, the **D**esigner, **E**verywhere, your **F**ather, **G**ood, the **H**ealer; I do the **I**mpossible; the **J**oy-giver, **K**ing of kings, **L**ove, a **M**ystery, **N**ever-ending, the **O**nly One, **P**ower; I **Q**uiet the storms; **R**eal, your **S**avior, **T**rustworthy, **U**nfailing, **V**oice, **W**isdom; fi**X** your eyes on heaven; I want to know **Y**ou; the A to **Z**!

Then I breathlessly ended with

"And all of that is who God says HE IS!"

Kaden looked at me and exclaimed,

"WOW!"

That's right, Kaden …WOW! This is your God.

And this is our God too, dear sisters and brothers. Wow!

A.W. Tozer, one of my favorite devotional writers said, "What comes into our minds when we think about God is the most important thing about us."[38]

Let's think about that. Amen.

<u>Your Name</u>
Your Name tells the story
Of Your love and the glory
Of Your sacrifice on the cross.

Your Name softly spoken
Heals hearts that have broken
In our lives of destruction and loss.

Your Name on our lips
Gives us peace when we slip
In this world where we're jostled and tossed.

Your Name opens floodgates
To rebuild and recreate
All that we thought we had lost.

You deserve love and glory
For what would be our story
If You hadn't suffered the cost?
        Penny Mandeville

<u>Prayer</u>

O glorious God, may we, Your children, be WOW-ed by You all our days. From A to Z, Your glory is revealed. May Your Son live and love through us to manifest Your glory all around. In Jesus' matchless and most Holy Name. Amen.

<u>Reflections</u>

1. Does your name have an interesting background or a particular meaning? Research it.
Are there any palindromes or other unusual features?

2. Thank the Lord for your unique story, manifest in your names.

3. What is the first thing that comes to your mind when you think about God?

4. Go through the alphabet and see if you can list your own description of God for each letter. Add in Scriptures to go with each, as you find them.

32. Yesterday…Tomorrow: Embracing Your Today

This is the day that the Lord has made;
let us rejoice and be glad in it.
Psalm 118:24 ESV

Are you a *futuring*-type person? Or as a friend of mine says, a *future-think*? Do you constantly project into the future? I do.

I'm not a procrastinator, so it is very difficult for me to live in the moment, in the *today*. My mind is always racing ahead—to the next responsibility, the next event, the next idea. As a result, "time crunches" and "performance anxiety" are the name of my game.

But all we really have is today, isn't it. Yesterday is gone. Tomorrow may not be ours. It's today or nothing.

And God is in our today. He is *I Am*. He was *I Am* when yesterday was today. He will be *I Am* when tomorrow becomes today. He was there when those hard and/or beautiful things happened in the past. He will be there for whatever lies ahead. Actually, He is already there, because He is *I Am*. And He is in the Eternal Present Tense.

What we usually do in our today is fight it, forget it, or just get through it. "After things settle down," we say. And we often like to think of the good ole days of the past. Remember the Beatles song. "Yesterday"?

"All our trouble seemed so far away…"[39]

Yeh, right. But those troubles were very real when yesterday was today. And God was there then, whether we realized it or not.

And then there's the song from Annie, "Tomorrow." I can't help loving the song because my sweet 5-year-old grandson Eli used to sing it to me.

> *"Tomorrow, tomorrow, I love ya, tomorrow, you're always a day away."*[40]

But God has given us today. So we need to embrace the real life we have today, not the life we wish we had. We experience our God in our here and now. And then we will be present to our loved ones, precious friends, and even strangers God sends our way. What a tragedy to miss what God has for us today.

So here are some reflections on TODAY:

1. TODAY is a gift. It's all we have…and it has been given to us by our Creator.

> This is the day which the LORD has made;
> Let us rejoice and be glad in it.
> Psalm 118:24 NASB

2. TODAY will never be again. It is totally unique with unique challenges and opportunities. Yesterday is gone…tomorrow is in the mind of God.

> What is your life? For you are a mist that appears for a little time and then vanishes. James 4:14 NASB

3. TODAY is filled with opportunities.

- The opportunity to "love on" those around us—our neighbors, our friends, our co-workers, our spouse, our children, our grandchildren, and others who may cross our path today.

> Carry each other's burdens, and in this way you will fulfill the law of Christ…Therefore, as we have opportunity, let us do good to all people...
> Galatians 6:2,10 NIV

Years ago, our kindergarten grandson Kaden learned that lesson well. One day, he said to his mom, "Did you know we each have an invisible bucket of happiness, and when we are mean, it is like dumping somebody's bucket?"

Kaden had just said "hi" to the neighbor and told his mom that he was filling up her bucket. Apparently, his teacher had just read, *Have You Filled a Bucket Today* by Carol McCloud.[41] Wow, maybe we need to go back to kindergarten.

Whose bucket can we fill today with just a little kindness?

- The opportunity to do our work with all the skill that God has put in us. There is great satisfaction in doing our work well, whether it's at home or at our job.

> Each of you should use whatever gift you have received to serve others, as faithful stewards of God's grace in its various forms. If anyone speaks, they should do so as one who speaks the very words of God. If anyone serves, they should do so with the

strength God provides, so that in all things God may be praised through Jesus Christ. To him be the glory and the power for ever and ever. Amen.
1 Peter 4:10-11 NIV

- The opportunity to walk with God, the Eternal I AM, in a deeper way.

> My sheep hear my voice, and I know them, and they follow me.
> John 10:27 NASB

Over the years, one of my favorite studies to teach from the Scriptures has been the Old Testament Names of God. In that study, one of the most exciting insights is that God's memorial name *Jehovah*, meaning *I AM*, expresses a God Who is eternally Present, totally above and beyond our chronological time, yet totally present in it with us and for us…*today*. And Jesus, the Son of God, uses that exact name, *I Am*…to describe Himself in the Gospel of John – *Jesus in Present Tense*.

So as you face *your today*, dear friend, may the realization of God's presence fill you with courage and excitement to embrace your today and live it for all it's worth.

> So teach us to number our days that we may get a heart of wisdom.
> Psalm 90:12

Today
Yesterday is past
Be thankful for lessons learned.

Tomorrow is uncertain.
Trust in Him at every turn.

But right now, this present moment
Is where your life is taking place!

So recognize He's with you now
Blessing you with His grace!
                              Penny Mandeville

<u>Prayer</u>
You belong to me, and I belong to You, TODAY, my God.
You live in Me, and I live in you, TODAY, my Lord.
You save me always, and You save me right NOW, my Savior!
You are Living Water for my thirsty soul right NOW.
You are my indwelling Peace, my ever-PRESENT Joy.
I embrace you, O God, in my TODAY. Teach me to look ahead,
even plan, without "going there" as if it all has to be done TODAY,
right NOW.
I rest in You, my indwelling PRESENT-Tense, Living Lord Jesus
Christ. So bring it on... Amen.

<u>Reflections</u>
1. Spend the week exploring Jesus' *I AM's* in the Gospel of John:

    ...the Bread of Life for your hungry heart in this moment
(John 6:35)

    ...the Light of your world today (John 8:12)

    ...the Door of the sheep whose sheep you are (John 10:7,9)

    ...your Good Shepherd for this situation (John 10:11-15)

    ...the Resurrection and your Life for your present emptiness
(John 11: 25)

…the Way, the Truth, and your Life for the path I you take right now (John 14:6)

…the True Vine in whom you are now abiding as a branch (John 15:1-5)

2. Journal the insights the Lord gives you.

3. Look for Glen Campbell's song "Today is Mine" on Youtube. You will be blessed as you rehearse your day through the amazing lyrics of this song.

Pooh, "What day is it?
"Today," said Piglet
"Ah", said Pooh,
"my favorite day."[42]
Winnie the Pooh

33. My Brother's Keeper: Loving Each Other Practically

Let brotherly love continue...
Hebrews 13:1

<u>"The Interpreter"—Understanding Each Other</u>

One day, I was driving grandsons, four-year old Evan and three-year old Carter, home after spending time with them at my house.

Carter said from his car seat in the back, "Babci (pronounced "BOB-chee," my Polish Grandma name), where we goin'?"

"I'm taking you home, hon'," I replied.

"I don't wanna go home. I wanna go Animal Wode," Carter said.

"Animal Road?" I asked.

"No, Animal <u>Wode</u>!" Carter emphasized.

"Animal Road?" I repeated. Then back and forth a couple of times.

Finally, Carter was in tears. So I turned to the "family interpreter," Evan.

"Evan, what is Carter saying?" I asked.

"He means 'Shade Wode,'" Evan replied.

"Shade Road?" I asked.

"No, Shade <u>Wode</u>!" Evan replied.

"Shade Road?" I repeated.

Now Evan was in tears, which is very unlike him. So I figured I just threw Evan over the edge also.

So I had an idea. "Evan, hon', use different words, like you usually do, to explain what you are saying."

This is the amazing thing Evan has done for a long time. He rarely gets frustrated if I don't understand. Evan patiently uses synonyms.

Evan thought and then said, "You know, it's by the Nike store far away."

I insisted, "I still don't know, honey. Animal Wode? Shade Wode? What is 'Wode'?"

Evan patiently replied, "You know, Babci, 'He's got the whole <u>wode</u> in His Hands.'"

I laughed and then cried. Here the first thing sweet little four-year old Evan thought of to explain the word "world" was a song he had learned about his Creator God, "He's got the whole world in His hands."

> Out of the mouth of infants and nursing babies, you have prepared praise.
> Matthew 21:16

By the way, the place Carter wanted to go to was "Traders ["Shade"] World ["Wode"]," a huge, crazy flea market with the statues of animals on the roof – thus, "Animal World."

"The Evangelist" – Caring for One Another

One day the boys were at my house. I had saved an awesome ad for them from a party store. It showed every costume imaginable and desirable to a three and four year old. But I couldn't find it. So we proceeded to search every room, but to no avail.

Finally, as a last resort, I prayed aloud, "Jesus, please find the ad."

Carter said, "Babci, Jesus isn't here!"

I replied, "Oh, hon,' He is. That's the beautiful thing. Jesus is everywhere."

Evan stepped in, "Carter, you know where ELSE He is?" Evan then very dramatically pointed to his little chest. "You need to get him in YOU. You need to pray."

Then to me, Evan said, "Carter doesn't have Him."

I picked up Carter and put him on my lap, thinking this might be the time to explain the gospel. Maybe little C is ready to "pray the sinner's prayer." So I began to tell him that inside his body is his real person, his heart.   He can ask Jesus to forgive his sins and come to live inside the real him.

Carter asked, "Inside my belly [pointing]? Then "Inside my bottom [pointing again with a giggle]?"

I figured by this time, things were deteriorating. So I turned to Evan, "I don't think Carter is ready yet. We need to pray for him."

> …And calling to him a child, he put him in the midst of them and said, "Truly, I say to you, unless you turn and become like children, you will never enter the kingdom of heaven. Whoever humbles himself like this child is the greatest in the kingdom of heaven.   Matthew 18:2-4 ESV

By the way, we did find the ad. Carter said to me, "In your purse, Babci?" Sure enough.

<u>"Siblings"-- Belonging to Each Other</u>

The parents of these little guys want them to grow up to be "best buds." They belong to each other. They are in the same "blood line," the same family.

And isn't that what our Father God desires for us His children -- that we would be devoted to one another ("best buds," so to speak)? No matter how much we disagree and even dislike each other, we are in the same "Blood Line," the same family.

> The way we know we've been transferred from death to life is that we love our brothers and sisters. … This is how we've come to understand and experience love: Christ sacrificed his life for us. This is why we ought to live sacrificially for

our fellow believers, and not just be out for ourselves.
1 John 3:14-16 MSG

We have a connection with each other that can't be broken, whether we like it or not. It's a connection as deep as union with each other in the Triune God. Just as in a human family, the primary connection a child has is with the parents (and thus with each other), so too in the family of God. Listen to how Jesus prayed the night before He died:

> I do not ask for these only, but also for those who will believe in me through their word, that they may all be one, just as you, Father, are in me, and I in you, that they also may be in us, so that the world may believe that you have sent me…we are one, I in them and you in me, that they may become perfectly one, so that the world may know that you sent me and loved them even as you loved me.
> John 17:20-23 ESV

<u>His Family</u>
How good it is to be
In Jesus' family.
Each branch is known
Because they love so much.

Their love for one another
Every sister and every brother
Wanting all the world
To feel God's gentle touch.
       Penny Mandeville

<u>Prayer</u>

Father, empower me through the indwelling Christ, Your Perfect Son, to love my brothers and sisters. Love them through me. Understand them through me. Care about their spiritual, emotional, physical welfare through me, O God. In Christ's Loving Name. Amen.

<u>Reflections</u>

As I've been meditating on my union with Christ and my brothers and sisters, I've revisited what are called "one another verses." There are many lists online. Start your own collection in your journal as you come across one that the Lord "highlights" for your attention. Ask Him about it and respond.

Today, know Christ more.
Grow in His Grace.
And go love each other like crazy.[43]
Mike Q. Daniel

GLORY IN THE HARD

Only by the grace of God
can we see control in the midst of chaos,
love in the midst of despair,
joy in the midst of sorrow.[44]
Mark & Patti Virkler
Counseled by God

34. Anxiety: Recognizing the Signal

…casting all your anxieties on him, because he cares for you.
1 Peter 5:6 ESV

I've always been prone to anxiety. As far back as I can remember, I have been nervous about all kinds of things — quizzes, tests, performances of any kind, up-coming unfamiliar events, putting my face in water, amusement park rides, and other "stupid stuff."

Then in motherhood, I feared my kids would be kidnapped. Or they would be "dead in a ditch" somewhere. Or I would die and some other woman (who didn't love them near as much as I) would raise them. You moms know we could go on and on.

Even as an adult teacher, I struggled -- whether it was teaching my kids in homeschool, or little ones in PK; adults in GED or ESOL classes, or Bible classes of various kinds. Nervousness, anxiety, and inadequacy would rear their ugly heads.

I've also found anxiety creeping up on me all of a sudden…not even provoked by conscious thoughts of one kind or another. Just seemingly out of the blue. I remember my homeopathic doctor telling me that the body has a "memory." Seemingly unprovoked, it can go into panic or anxiety on its own.

And lately, because of fatigue, age-related physical issues (dizziness, vertigo), a fall, or family stresses, anxiety can come on me "all of a sudden" -- even sometimes in the middle of the night. So I am getting re-schooled by my Abba Father God on what to do when this happens.

Long ago, I quit beating myself up for being nervous and anxious. I went through a horrible period of panic/anxiety attacks when I was a young mom. And the worst part of it all was that I thought God was punishing me for not "doing" the Christian life perfectly. On top of that, I judged myself severely for even having the panic attacks to begin with. After all, mature, spiritual Christians don't have anxiety attacks. That must mean I'm not trusting God (or so I very wrongly thought). But it was in the midst of it all God gave me a Scripture. The Holy Spirit used it to deliver me from those attacks and set my heart free:

> When I am afraid, I will put my trust in Thee.
> Psalm 56:3 NASB

Did you notice that first word? *WHEN!* Not *IF*, not "shame on you." If.

God knows that I will be *afraid, nervous, anxious.* This is a scary world with lots of dangers. But what He did then was give me the key, a signal (so to speak)…

> "My Child, when you feel that anxiety, fear, nervousness, use it as a signal to turn to ME. Focus on ME, not the anxiety."

And so I did … over and over; time after time. And I was free.

And now in my current, spontaneous, even middle of the night, early morning anxiousness, God has met me again through His indwelling Holy Spirit. The Scripture that sets me free now is one that the Lord taught me years ago, but lately it has taken on a new urgency and desperation. The Holy Spirit reminds me I have the mind of Christ.

So even in my waking thoughts, I automatically go to my Abba
Father God

…casting all my anxieties on Him

Why? *…because He cares for me …*

Little ole anxiety-prone me.

As I respond to the signal, He takes my anxieties and bears them and
sets me free. And He will do that for you too, my friend. He will
meet you there right IN your anxiety, panic, nervousness. He will
speak His words of truth into your mind and soul and body.

Don't beat yourself up. Don't try to carry it on your own. See your
anxiety as a signal to turn to Him, run to Him, cast your stuff on
Him, because He cares for little ole anxiety prone you too.

<u>Anxiety</u>
What I notice about anxiety
Is that it's a made-up reality.

On this unreal day of my imagination
Jesus isn't there, cause it's my own creation.

But when this day of worry does arrive
Of course, He's right there by my side!

I must remember Jesus will always be
My peace, my rest, my serenity.
       Penny Mandeville

<u>Prayer</u>

Father, You are so gracious to rescue me in my distress. You are there even in my anxiety, waiting to reveal Yourself as I respond to the "signal" to turn to You. Thank You that I don't have to beat myself up and try to carry it on my own. Remind me, by your Indwelling Holy Spirit, to cast all my anxiety on You because you care for me—little ole anxiety prone me. In Jesus Name.

<u>Reflections</u>

1. Do you have chronic trouble with anxiety? Has the Lord already given you truth to hang onto from His Word, by His Spirit? Be sure to record that in your journal.

2. Write out the verses and truth from this selection. Meditate on each. Ask the Holy Spirit to highlight a verse or a word to your heart and life to serve as your signal.
Then when anxiety begins, don't condemn yourself. Let that word be your "go to" when you feel the anxiety coming on. Run to Him. He will see you through.

35. Crisis: Balancing Acceptance and Hope

For we know that all creation has been groaning
as in the pains of childbirth right up to the present time.
And we believers also groan, even though we have the Holy Spirit
within us as a foretaste of future glory,
for we long for our bodies to be released from sin and suffering.
We, too, wait with eager hope for the day when God will give us our
full rights as his adopted children,
including the new bodies he has promised us.
We were given this hope when we were saved.

Romans 8:22-25 NLT

I live in Ohio. And in the early days of the COVID pandemic our governor had a daily news conference every weekday. During one of those conferences, the state director of health shared a beautiful nugget of emotional and spiritual health. Referring to a favorite book by a Holocaust survivor, she shared two things which helped those victims survive the extreme crisis. And she believed those same two things could help us survive the pandemic crisis. They are "accepting our present reality" and "holding on to hope" at the same time.

My ears perked up, because I believe this is Truth with a capital T. In fact, I remember coming to the realization years ago, when my kids were still small, that I was spending a lot of emotional energy fighting my own life. I was resisting my present, real-life circumstances. They centered around mysterious allergic reactions that defied understanding. Round and round went agonizing thoughts:

- Why do I have to live in OHIO when my health would be better in the desert and mountains of AZ or the coastline of NJ?
- Why do I have these exotic allergies and sensitivities and mysterious reactions?
  Surely this is not God's will.

How stupid was that—to fight against my own life? I finally realized that God wanted me to embrace my life, hug it to my breast, thank God for it, brokenness and all, and yes, Ohio and all.

What peace, what fullness unfolded for me—though my state of residence and the state of my health didn't change. It didn't mean I couldn't still hope for a cure or hope that the end would come to my suffering. But I needed to embrace my present reality instead of fight against it.

Paul's statement became a mantra for me,

> By the grace of God I am what I am, and his grace toward me was not in vain.
> 1 Corinthians 15:10 ESV

That reminded me of the story of a woman who had fought her own life, Catherine Marshall, wife of Chaplain of the Senate, Rev. Peter Marshall (1947-49).   She was a woman who recognized the Lord speaking to her mind and heart, both through the Scriptures and the Spirit. Catherine spoke of hearing the Lord and following Him. And more importantly, she spoke of coming to what she called *the relinquishment of her will to the Lord.*

In the midst of a stubborn case of TB that wouldn't yield to prayer or medical intervention, Catherine finally came to the point of wanting the Lord more than wanting healing.

In Catherine's own words:

> This is my situation at the moment. I'll face the reality of it. But I'll also accept willingly whatever a loving Father sends.
>
> Acceptance, therefore, never slams the door on hope. Yet even with hope our relinquishment must be the real thing, because this giving up of self-will is the hardest thing we human beings are ever called on to do.[45]

What about you, dear brothers and sisters? Can you sincerely say, "By the grace of God, I am what I am" and "I am, where I am" and "this is, what it is"?

Are you embracing fully what God has for you right here and right now? For some of us our present circumstances are more serious than others. No matter. The acceptance of our present reality is not just for crisis situations. It's for every today (crisis or mundane) that we have on this earth. Each of our moments is important to us and to Him.

There's a certain acceptance of one's life that characterizes the person who lives by faith. And oh, what peace and joy will be ours. Justin Gravitt stated that we can walk through crisis (speaking of the pandemic) in one of three ways:

We can distract ourselves from it.
We can deny it.
Or we can dwell in it.[46]

Brothers and sisters, let's dwell in our present situation and embrace our today as God's will for our individual lives. And the beauty of it all is that we will meet Him right there in the midst—the easy and the hard and everything in-between—every "today" of our lives. And that is our greatest hope of all.

> . . . I've loved you the way my Father has loved me. Make yourselves at home [dwell] in my love . . . Live in me. Make your home [dwell] in me just as I do in you. John 15:9 MSG

<u>My Path</u>
There are things in this life
That are hard to accept.
My days would be smoother
Without their effect.

But I trust them to be
Part of Your plan.
A plan that I often
Don't understand.

But if You can accept
The things I have done.
Then I must accept
The path that I'm on.

For Your love and forgiveness
Help me to cope.

And there, My Sweet Jesus,
Is where I find HOPE.
        Penny Mandeville

<u>Prayer</u>
Lord Jesus, You are truly my Home. I sink down deep into my place
in You, and I am at peace. Whether crisis or mundane, suffering or
comfort, my Hope is You. Remind me Who You are today and
Whose I am as I go through my day. In Your Name. Amen.

<u>Reflections</u>
1. Look at 1 Peter 5:6-11 and Romans 15:13. Journal what He shows
you and yield your struggles into His Almighty care because…He
cares for you.

2. What are God's instructions and encouragement in the midst of
suffering?

Occasionally weep deeply over the life you hoped would be.
Grieve the losses. Then wash your face. Trust God.
And embrace the life you have.[47]
        John Piper

36. C-C-Courage: Counting on the Courageous Christ

For in Christ all the fullness of the Deity lives in bodily form,
and in Christ you have been brought to fullness.
Colossians 2:9-10a NASB

Who doesn't love the classic movie *The Wizard of Oz*? And of all the characters, the Cowardly Lion is a favorite. Why is that, I wonder? Could it be that we see ourselves in him? While putting on a brave front to face life, we find that in reality we are scared little kitties inside.

I especially love the lion's courage monologue:

> COWARDLY LION: *Courage!* What makes a king out of a slave? *Courage!* What makes the flag on the mast to wave? *Courage!* What makes the elephant charge his tusk in the misty mist, or the dusky dusk? What makes the muskrat guard his musk? *Courage!* What makes the sphinx the seventh wonder? *Courage!* What makes the dawn come up like thunder? *Courage!* What makes the Hottentot so hot? What puts the "ape" in apricot? What have they got that I ain't got?

> DOROTHY, SCARECROW, TINMAN: *Courage!*

> COWARDLY LION: You can say that again![48]

Can you identify? I can. And that's how I felt with teaching and speaking in front of people. I was inwardly terrified. I felt a lot of shame about this, because I wanted to trust God completely. I've since found out, though, that speaking in public is one of the top fears among women—go figure.

As one pundit has put it, "According to most studies, people's number one fear is public speaking. Number two is death. Death is number two… This means to the average person, if you go to a funeral, you're better off in the casket than doing the eulogy."[49]

To me this fear was no laughing matter. It had become debilitating, to the point of physical illness. This was especially true when it came to a big meeting connected to my job with a local Christian school. I used to be a homeschool coordinator, and in those early days, I had a very large group of families to help. At the end of the summer each year, we would meet as a group with all our families— new and returning. At that time, we would tell them about ourselves, encourage them, and explain how the program ran.

Well, I dreaded it. Not because they were a hostile group—in fact the opposite was true. They loved me, and I felt their love. So in my mind, this fear was totally illogical and unfounded. I talked to myself and the Lord about it, but to no avail. It would ruin my whole summer every year! Until . . .

One summer, I was agonizing as usual over the big home school meeting. In the midst of my agony, I thought to myself, "I need courage." So I proceeded to beg, plead, pray for courage. I tried to do my best "courage self-talk." I was still a wreck.

In the meantime, that summer I happened to be teaching the little book of Colossians for the second time (I'm a slow learner). As I was preparing to teach, the Holy Spirit highlighted several verses to my mind and heart: "*Christ in you*, the hope of glory. . .For *in Him* [Christ] all the fullness of Deity [God] dwells in bodily form, and *in*

Him you have been made complete [Gk. *full*]"
Colossians 1:27; 2:9–10 NASB (emphasis added).

All of a sudden, the realization came crashing through.

- Jesus wasn't a wimp. Remember how he stood up to the Pharisees—not exactly a friendly audience.
- Courage is part of the fullness of God in Christ.
- The courageous Christ lives in me. He will live his courageous life through me as I trust him.

That's what being *filled in him* means. No more begging, pleading, self-talk, Christian mental mind games. No more shame and despair.

So I decided to trust the courageous Christ. And guess what? He *was* courageous in and through me so that I could relax and be my "charming" self—to the glory of God. And I now know,

> *Every situation is a new opportunity to trust the full Christ who dwells within.*

He will be who He is, in and through you also, each day in every circumstance of your life.

So do you need courage today?
The *courageous Christ* is courageous in you and will be courageous through you as you trust him.

Do you need love, forgiveness, patience, ___________ today?
The full Christ lives within you. He is full in you and will be whatever you need through you as you trust Him.

It's the devil's lie to get you to think of yourself as separate from your Lord. He's not up there, and you're down here, praying He throws down a little *courage* (or whatever) if you pray correctly. No. You are one with Him, united in a way that nothing in heaven and earth can separate.

> I have been crucified [united] *with* Christ; and it is no longer I who live, but Christ lives in me; and the life which I now live in the flesh I live by faith in the Son of God, who loved me and gave Himself up for me.
> Galatians 2:20 NASB

So, dear sisters and brothers, look at whatever you are facing today as your opportunity to experience Him in his fullness in and through you. Praise his Holy Name.

<u>He's All We Need</u>
Jesus is our storehouse.
He's all we'll ever need.
His Spirit is inside us
To guide when we concede.

He's there to give us courage
When we are afraid.
He comforts us and gives us hope
When we have been betrayed.

He'll share with us His patience
When ours is almost gone.
Because He shows us His forgiveness
We'll forgive what others've done.

He gives us Holy Wisdom
When we become confused.
He gives us strength to stand our ground
When we have been abused.

He cares for us and loves us
So we can love the lost.
He reminds us how He saved us
And just how much it cost.
   Penny Mandeville

<u>Prayer</u>

My courageous Christ, Lord of all fullness. You are everything I could ever need. Keep me from turning to false fillers and counterfeit helpers and my own bankrupt self-effort to meet my need in the moment. We are never separate…always one. Thank you, in Your Sufficient Name. Amen.

<u>Reflections</u>

1. If you are familiar with the story of *The Wizard of Oz*, answer these questions:

- What is the need of each character in *The Wizard of Oz*?
- How does Jesus fill each of those needs? Search the Scriptures about each of the needs.
- Which character can you identify with?

2. Cry out to the Lord, praying about your needs. Use the "fill in the blank" if that is helpful.

37. *That Was for This:* Learning to Hear God

My sheep hear My voice,
and I know them, and they follow Me
John 10:27 NASB

At my mother's knee, I listened to stories she would read from our big family Bible. You know the one—with the fragile, "holy" pages and glossy, colored pictures scattered throughout. And of course, pages that recorded our family's religious history—births and deaths, marriages and baptisms, first communions and confirmations.

"This is God's book," Mom would tell me. "His words and stories are here for us."

But it wasn't until my young adulthood, that I became aware I could also hear God speak to me in the still, small Voice of His Spirit within. And there were times in my life when I heard Him "ahead of time," so to speak. I call those times a *"that was for this"* situation.

One significant time was when I was preparing to teach a retreat workshop on living by faith from the letter to the Hebrews, chapters 11 & 12. This section of Scripture speaks of Old Testament people who lived by faith by focusing on the unseen God. The passage culminates with the encouragement for us to live by faith today, fixing our eyes on Jesus.

As I was preparing for this retreat, I immersed myself in these chapters. But one passage jumped out at me and grab my attention time after time. I couldn't get away from it:

> ...<u>by faith [they]</u> conquered kingdoms, performed acts of
> righteousness, obtained promises, …Women received back
> their dead by resurrection ...
> <u>and others</u> were tortured, not accepting their release, so that
> they might obtain a better resurrection…
> <u>And all these</u>...gained approval through their faith...
> Hebrews 11:33-39 NASB (emphasis mine).

So good things happened to people who lived by faith. But also bad things happened to people who lived by faith. What a revelation. I had naively expected as a Christian, if I lived by faith, things would turn out right. But not according to this passage. And I couldn't get away from it.

At the end of the retreat, I drove the hour home from Cincinnati to Dayton. I kept asking myself, "Why can't I get out of Hebrews 11? Why can't I move on?"

Just then the revelation of the Holy Spirit interrupted my churning thoughts. "Oh no. God is preparing me for something big, and it's going to be 'bad.'"

Sure enough, when I walked through the door that evening, some health issues with my then 20-year-old son Jeremy had gone from bad to worse. What had started out as an abscessed tooth weeks before, now pointed to a suspicious swollen area in his neck. Months before, this "swelling" was diagnosed as "swollen lymph nodes." But he needed a biopsy.

My mind and emotions started going crazy. "How could this be happening to my beautiful, healthy, athletic son?

"This was the same son I prayed for, gave birth to, sang hymns to, taught Scriptures to, read to, cried over, laughed with, …

"This was the sweet little boy who would smell my coffee at 5:00am and show up smiling at 5:15, joining me in my early morning devotions.

"This was the little guy who would sing to me about God's love when he saw me crying.

 "And he is that same artistic, sensitive, affectionate, funny, basketball-loving 'little boy' whom we were now launching into adulthood.

"So how could this be happening?"

As I waited to hear the result of the biopsy, I had a sense it wasn't going to be good. And sure enough, thyroid cancer. To say the diagnosis was an incredible shaking to all our hearts and souls is an understatement.

But then in the throes of all the pain and ripping apart of this mama's heart, I remembered God's *that was for this*—good things happen to people of faith but also bad things happen to people of faith. And the only way to make it through is to focus on Christ, trusting Him in the midst of the suffering,

> "…fixing [my] eyes on Jesus the Author and Perfector of faith." Hebrews 12:1-2 NASB

Later the realization came—God had also prepared our son. Months before Jeremy's cancer diagnosis, he and I had an interesting conversation when I picked him up for the weekend at Grace College.

As we were driving the several hours home, Jeremy told me, "Mom, I keep hearing the same Bible verse almost everywhere I go—in chapel, on Christian radio, in the dorm, in class …"

> I can do all things through him who strengthens me. Philippians 4:13 ESV

I assured him, "Jeremy, that sounds like God. That's how He often speaks to us."

Jeremy was wondering what this could be about. Maybe trying the college basketball team again? Something about classes? Relationships? Not sure.

Months later, but not long after Jeremy's cancer diagnosis, I remembered his verse, Philippians 4:13. "Aha, that was God's 'for this.'"

And so I said to him, "Jeremy, remember the verse the Lord gave you months ago, Philippians 4:13? Well, I woke up this morning, sensing the Lord wanted me to tell you '*that was for this*' trial in your life."

As the days and months of surgery and healing went by, God did empower Jeremy to walk through the trial of his young life with grace, courage, and the strength of an Almighty Savior in the midst of suffering.

As Jeremy said, "I'm scared, but trusting God."

What about you, dear friend? Is there a Scripture that is coming at you in many ways: in song, in preaching, on Christian radio, in your daily devotional reading? Is there a recurring thought that sounds like God and His ways?

"Take the risk" (trust) that God is speaking directly to you. He may be strengthening you by speaking comfort, truth, empowerment, preparation, and even *that was for this*—whatever is needed, to your listening heart.

This is what it means to live by faith.

<u>He Speaks to Me</u>
Lord, when you speak to me
You make my heart rejoice.
May I hear You very clearly
Above all the world's loud noise.

There are times when I read your word
Something leaps into my heart.
And I know there is a message there
You're wanting to impart.

And I've had dreams and visions
Where You've revealed Your will for me.
I listen for I know You know
What I cannot foresee.

At times You choose to speak to me
Through someone else's words.
Please give me the discernment to
Know their words are Yours.

Often it's just a feeling
That will suddenly appear.
At times my mind ignores You
But my heart will always hear.

So thank You for how You speak to us
In whatever way is Your choice.
I pray we'll always listen
And recognize Your voice.
        Penny Mandeville

<u>Prayer</u>

O Shepherd of our Souls, thank you that we are Your sheep, so we can hear and recognize the voice of our Shepherd. Teach us to hear You every day of our lives. In Your Name. Amen.

<u>Reflections</u>

1. What does God's voice sound like to you? God speaks love and grace and truth.
He may be speaking to you in your "love language."

2. Is there a repeated, recurring message through Scripture, song, people, situations? Journal His words to you.

38. Archaeological Dig: Trusting the Rock that Follows

... and all drank the same spiritual drink,
for they were drinking from a spiritual rock which followed them;
and the rock was Christ.
1 Corinthians 10:4 NASB

Our daughter Beth was an art history major in college. One day she received an unusual opportunity. The visiting professor of her archaeology class invited Beth to join a group of college students from around the country for an archaeological dig in Sicily the following summer. This honor came as a result of her quality research done on a special project in the class. And the exciting part was the group would be going to the exact "excavation" she had researched.

Beth was excited. But it freaked me out! I was totally overwhelmed at the thought of my daughter going that far away from home with no one I knew and probably with no mature Christians. But I had been learning through some serious health crises of my children to entrust them totally to the Lord. So Beth applied to the university for a grant to fund the trip. And we prayed for God's will to be done. I knew it would be foolish to stand in the way of God's will for her life.

Well guess what? Not only did she get the grant, but the university offered her more money than what she applied for. Now what college ever does that? To me, it was a confirmation that the Lord was in this no matter how terrified I was.

In the meantime, an obscure verse captured my mind and imagination while I was doing my Bible study. Writing of the Israelites traveling through the wilderness, Paul says,

Our fathers were all under the cloud and all passed through the sea; and all were baptized into Moses in the cloud and in the sea; and all ate the same spiritual food; and all drank the same spiritual drink, for they were drinking from *a spiritual rock which followed them; and the Rock was* Christ.
1 Corinthians 10:1–4 NASB (emphasis added).

I had never really noticed that verse before. What did that mean – *"the Rock that followed them was Christ?"* I would soon find out.

Back to Beth: she was going. I was praying and trusting. At our small group Bible study just days before her departure, we were worshipping the Lord, singing the beautiful song "Faithful One" by Brian Doerksen. These lyrics grabbed me:

> *Faithful One, so unchanging . . .*
> *You're my Rock of Peace . . .*
> *My hope is in You alone*

The Lord spoke to my heart,

> "I will be the Rock that follows Beth from Columbus to NYC to Rome to Sicily, all around Sicily and wherever she travels, back to Rome, to NYC, to Columbus, and safely home again."

The God of Peace came over me. So a few days later, we took Beth to the Columbus airport, and I freely and confidently entrusted her to her Rock. And whenever I emailed Beth or talked to her, I said, "Remember the Rock that follows you."

When Beth returned, she told us of a time when she ended up at the end of the bus line. It was dark, and she had to follow the coastline of the sea to make her way back to her apartment. She said, "I was scared but I sensed a Presence."

… Because *the* Rock *that followed Beth was Christ.*

Let me encourage you, dear brothers and sisters, moms and dads, grandmas and grandpas -- the Lord is our Rock. And He not only follows us. He follows each of our loved ones -- He has their backs and ours. When anxieties arise over their welfare, remind yourself and remind them that the <u>Rock</u> that follows them is the Lord Jesus Christ. Entrust yourself and them to our Lord Jesus Christ, our faithful, loving, strong <u>Rock</u>.

<u>You Are with Them</u>
Unsure and afraid
Of the choices they've made
Can lead me to despair.

But then I remember
Your voice so tender
Telling me you'll always be there.

You're the rock behind them
The fire that refines them
The water that cleanses their soul.

You're the wisdom that guides them
The wind that revives them
The Love that swallows them whole.
      Penny Mandeville

<u>Prayer</u>
O faithful and strong Rock. Thank You that You are the Stabilizer, the Protector of my life…and the lives of those I so desperately love and care about. Be the Rock that follows _____________ today, wherever they go. Protect them and manifest Your Almighty Presence. In Your amazing Name, our solid Rock. Amen.

<u>Reflections</u>
1. Read Psalm 23 and underline or record in your journal the verses that speak of your Shepherd's loving presence in your life and the life of your loved one.

2. Do the same for Psalm 139.
Is there any place where He is not there with you and your loved one?

3. If you have access to *YouTube* on an electronic device, do a search for the song "Where Can I Go" by GLAD. Rest in the realization of His presence every step of your life.

Where can I go from Your Spirit
And where can I hide from Your love
When I am hurting
It comforts me to know
Nothing can take away Your love
Nothing can take Your love[50]
GLAD

GLORY IN ACTIVITY

*The rule is you have to dance a little bit
in the morning before you leave the house
because it changes the way
you walk out in the world.*[51]
Sandra Bullock

39. Walkin' n Talkin': Journeying with Jesus

He has told you, O man, what is good;
and what does the Lord require of you
but to do justice, and to love kindness,
and to walk humbly with your God?
Micah 6:8 ESV

My grandson Carter and I had this thing going that we called "walkin-n-talkin 'n' talkin-n-walkin." It was pure delight for both of us, because Carter was 3½ and I'm Carter's *Babci* (Polish for Grandma). I knew that it wouldn't last forever, and he'd grow up and become interested in many other things. But for the time, we had each other and walkin-n-talkin 'n' talkin-n-walkin!

Well, what was walkin-n-talkin 'n' talkin-n-walkin? It was simply this: we just walked (or trotted if you're Carter) and chatted up a storm at a local, enclosed shopping area. What did we talk about? Anything and everything, from the mundane to the sublime—from blue ugly dolls to how many "frosties" (snowmen) did we see, to which one we liked best (mine was the one with the plaid scarf, his was the one with the sparkly colors), or whether the train would be running in the children's department of the shoe store.

Carter and I talked about how we loved each other and how we were best buds. We also talked about how God wants him to obey mommy and daddy, and how Jesus living in him obeys through him (explained in 3-year-old talk). And of course, we ate burgers and played games in our booth at Buffalo Wild Wings®. What glorious days.

My time with Carter reminds me of another pair of walkers and talkers: Jesus and His disciples. They walked and talked everywhere together—through grain fields, through vineyards, from one town to another to another, and even out on the water, chatting up a storm. Of course, Jesus being the Rabbi did the most significant talking. But the disciples chatted too. Sometimes they put their foot in their mouths, like asking who would be the greatest in the kingdom. But that was okay because Jesus loved them anyway. They were best buds.

Perhaps my favorite walk of theirs is the one on the road to Emmaus right after Jesus' resurrection (Luke 24). The two disciples didn't even recognize that it was their Lord Jesus Christ that was walking with them. And He was sharing the Scriptures with them that spoke of himself and his death, burial, and resurrection. It wasn't until the intimate activity of eating together that their eyes were opened to know him as their outdoor companion.

I think it's the same with us present-day disciples of Jesus. We often go our merry way feeling like the Lord is up there somewhere sending down a little help if we ask. But in reality, He is with us at all times.

A while ago, I was going through an emotionally rough time. I felt confused and disheartened and lonely. I decided to go for a walk through a beautiful senior center near our home. As I walked, I moaned and groaned to myself, "Nobody really knows me. Nobody really cares. Nobody really gets who I am."

I sat down on the grass in a grove of trees, feeling all alone. Then came the still, small Voice of my unseen Walking Partner, "Nobody really knew Me. Nobody really cared for Me. Nobody really got who I am. Only My heavenly Father."

It was then that I realized I hadn't been walking and moaning alone. So the rest of the way, I walked hand-in-hand with the Lonely One.

What about you, my dear brothers and sisters in Christ? Do you realize that you have a life Walking Partner who is your Almighty Loving Lord Jesus Christ? You are never alone, and you are always understood and cherished. No matter what you're going through, walk through it hand-in-hand with your Savior. Listen for the quiet Voice of your speaking Lord.

He Knows Me

Who knows me both inside and out?
Who loves me even when I doubt?
Who's with me when I feel alone?
Who tells me I'm His very His own?
Who forgives me when I stumble and fall?
Who is with me even before I call?

Jesus knows me both inside and out.
Jesus loves me even when I doubt.
Jesus is with me when I feel alone.
Jesus tells me I'm His very own.
Jesus forgives me when I stumble and fall.
Jesus is with me even before I call.
      Penny Mandeville

Prayer

Lord Jesus, thank You for walking with me every step of my life. Thank You that You get me and what I am going through. Open my eyes to Your Presence with me at all times. Remind me that I am never alone. In Your Awesome Name. Amen.

<u>Reflections</u>
1. Today (and perhaps every week during this study), why not go "walkin-n-talkin" with your Savior, listening to Him, thanking Him, and getting His perspective on what's going on in your life right now.

2. You could go to a nature area, an enclosed mall, anywhere the two of you can be together. Pour out your heart and let Him fill you with His peace, presence, and life-giving words.
Envision yourself walking with Him hand-in-hand, even through your darkest of valleys. Remember: "A person who walks with God is always moving in the right direction."[52]

40. The Race: Accepting Your Unique Life

…let's run with endurance the race that is set before us,
looking only at Jesus, the originator and perfecter of the faith …
Hebrews 12: 1-2 NASB

I was never athletic as a child or young person. My six siblings all were. My two sisters were cheerleaders, and my four brothers were baseball and basketball players. Then there was me -- ever the student, me. I never even learned to swim. So as I look back, how did I ever become a runner?

Now let me describe what I mean by "runner." When John and I were first married and living in Pennsylvania, I took up running stairs. I had read an article on "Aerobics for Women" which listed various exercises with charts to reach an optimal level of fitness. And I was also hoping to stay skinny. The only exercise feasible for me, no matter the weather in that hilly area, was stair running. And so I began, even running in the married students' dorm stairwell when we were in Bible school in Chicago.

Then I ran outside through my first pregnancy (what a sight, huh?). A few years later, I ran through a second pregnancy (very slowly toward the end) in Dallas when John was in seminary.

That's when I entered my first race. Dallas Seminary had a 5K every year. With fear and trepidation, I decided to enter the newly formed "women's division" of the race. And guess what? I won. OK, now I have to confess -- no other women entered the race. So I was the only runner.

Now let me fast forward several years. I kept on running while I was homeschooling our kids through elementary and middle school. And this is where my story slows down.

Keep in mind my husband John is athletic – he had run track and was a basketball star in high school and a life guard at the community pool. He sincerely (not critically) tried to help me improve my technique in running. He pointed out my stride was "too choppy." So I tried to follow his suggestions but always defaulted to my comfortable choppiness.

One day during our usual homeschool recess time, the kids and I went to the track behind our community middle school. I could run and my homeschool kids could play. Rarely was anyone on the tract during the day…except for one "fateful" day. All of a sudden, in the midst of my running and my kids' playing, a male PE teacher emerged onto the track followed by his class of middle school PE students.

"Oh my goodness, please God, not middle school students."

The teacher directed the students to the bleachers. As they were taking their seats, I self-consciously ran past. The teacher continued to instruct them. Then the students took off onto the track running in small groups – some running past me and some staying behind.

As I ran around the track ready to pass the teacher again, he said to me, "I'm using you as an example for my students on how to run."

I was stunned. I said, "You mean how NOT to run. My husband says my stride is too choppy."

The teacher replied, "Oh no. Your stride is just perfect."

I was stunned! I continued running …

"My stride is perfect? Really? Unathletic me…perfect?"

And here I was trying to change my natural style of running because of what I considered an expert opinion. I had felt a failure. But I had been running well all along.

In the following days, my favorite running passage of Scripture came to mind.

> Therefore, since we also have such a great cloud of witnesses surrounding us,
> let's rid ourselves of every obstacle and the sin which so easily entangles us, and
> let's run with endurance <u>the race that is set before us</u>,
> <u>looking only at Jesus</u>, the originator and perfecter of the faith
> … Hebrews 12:1-2 NASB

This little phrase jumped out at me, "the race that is <u>set before</u> us [<u>me</u>]." My own unique race that no one else can run. And how do I do that? "Looking <u>only</u> at <u>Jesus</u>."
Not looking at well-meaning people, like my husband whose heart was in the right place;
Not comparing myself with others, even godly people I admire;
Not trying to meet up to other's expectations;
Not focusing on keeping important others OK;
Not working my way down the latest Christian checklist.

These and many other traps are the "obstacles" that will pull me off the track every time. Only Jesus, who lives within me…only Him -- in me and through me, as me – not as some "faux-me."

I think of the apostle Paul who could have really been insecure with all his past failures in "serving God." He could have tried to copy the other "apostles." But no. I love what he said,

> But <u>by the grace of God I am what I am</u>, and His grace toward me did not prove vain; but I labored even more than all of them<u>, yet not I, but the grace of God with me</u>
> 1 Corinthians 15:10 NASB (emphasis added).

So it really is all grace. I am who I am. I can rest in that, with all my idiosyncrasies and unique style and personality and weaknesses and strengths. Because He is who He is. And He is in me and through me, as me. Glory to you, Jesus.

What about you, dear brothers and sisters? Are you trying hard to be something you are not. Grab hold of the race, the life, that is set before you and run with all your heart in your own unique style. You and Jesus together – He is in you and through you, as you.

Let Him do that by faith.

<u>Running My Race</u>
God made me to run the race
That is uniquely me.

It's the only way that I can be
All that I'm meant to be.

He doesn't equip me
To run your race.

And you're not equipped
To run mine.

Trying to be someone I'm not
Goes against how I'm defined.

So I'll run my race
And you run yours.

And I think that
We will find

That life will flow
The way it should go

According to
His perfect design.
> Penny Mandeville

<u>Prayer</u>

Lord Jesus, Runner par Excellence, I fix my eyes on You. Thank You that You fashioned me to run together with You as me. May that ever be true, O glorious God. In Your Name. Amen.

<u>Reflections</u>

1. Look at:

> *For we are God's masterpiece. He has created us anew in Christ Jesus, so we can do the good things he planned for us long ago.* Ephesians 2:10 NLT

2. How would GOD describe you, His masterpiece?

3. How would GOD describe the "good things" HE created you to do?

4. Now embrace your "race" for the gift that it is. Live it with all that is in you. Thank your Creator.

41. The Swim Meet: Focusing on the Goal

Do you not know that those who run in a race all run,
but only one receives the prize?
Run in such a way that you may win.
1 Corinthians 9:4 NASB

Summer break is the time every child looks forward to -- lazy days: no school and homework, playing outside with friends, sleeping in. What glory. Glory that is, until parents' plans for a productive summer come into play.

Several years, those "productive plans" put our grandsons Evan and Carter on the swim team at their local swim club. Mind you, their parents didn't have great ambitions for them, just that they would become stronger swimmers.

Valid, right? Right, but not to the boys because of two things:

- Early morning swim team practices. And when I say early, I mean early timewise, but also "cold-morning-air-wise" and "cold-water-wise."

- Competitions with other swim clubs. Carter in particular was not fond of this at all. When I say not fond, I mean "could-care-less-about-winning."

In fact, Carter himself just cared about two things:

- Getting one of each color ribbon, which would mean he would have to place first, second, third, and even last. Did I mention that Carter is an artist?

- And this was most important -- Who would be there to watch him swim: Mom and Dad, Grandma and Grandpa, Babci & Poppi, and big brother Evan?

So every time Carter was "racing," instead of focusing on the finish line and trying to win, Carter looked from side to side. He was looking to see if Mom & Dad, Grandma and Grandpa, Babci and Poppi, and Evan were all watching.

But the coach and the crowd (including us) wanted Carter and his team to win. So I had an idea. When I was at Carter's next swim meet, I knew he was going to be looking along the sidelines to see if all of us were watching. So I decided to get at the end of the lane where he was "racing." I crouched down low trying to catch his eye. Then I began calling and beckoning to him,

"Carter…come on, swim, swim. This way!"

And guess what. He won first place.

So after that, we all piled up at the end of his lane and beckoned, calling out to him,

"Swim, Carter, swim. Here…this way!"

And he kept winning.

I smile every time I think of Carter's "swimming career." He did become a strong swimmer that summer. And he may even have learned to focus on the "goal."

But I also smile because I can just picture Jesus, beckoning to us,

> "Here…to Me. Focus. I AM your Goal. Don't worry about who is watching, who is approving, who is achieving. Don't be concerned about getting the 'colored ribbons of pseudo-success' that seem so important right now.
> Follow Me. I am your Goal."

This reminds me of the interchange that took place between the resurrected Jesus and Peter at the breakfast on the beach (John, chapter 21). Jesus had just commissioned Peter to "shepherd His flock." Then He told Peter by what kind of death he would glorify God. Jesus concluded with the invitation, "Follow Me." But that wasn't the end of the conversation.

> Peter turned around and saw the disciple whom Jesus loved following them… So Peter, upon seeing him, said to Jesus, "Lord, and what about this man?"
> Jesus said to him, "If I want him to remain until I come, what is that to you? You follow Me."   John 21:21-22 NASB

Oh, how we do look all around us, wonder who is watching. And we compare ourselves to those onlookers -- others in the family of God. We end up disheartened, because of another's opportunities or success. We become jealous or prideful – jealous, if the other person is "better than us" or prideful, if we happen to be doing better. We stay locked up inside, instead of free in our walk with Christ.

But in the midst of all our angst and faulty focus, Jesus is continually saying to us,

> "Here…this way…What is that to you? You follow Me."

Brothers and sisters, just follow Him. He is our Goal. Let's get our eyes off the "sidelines" and the "prizes." Let's follow Him.

<u>Winning the Race</u>
In this life we've been given, this life we are living
We sometimes compete with ourselves.

Let's avoid the distractions of all the attractions
Of lesser things in which to delve.

Lord, put blinders on me, free me from what binds me
Keep me focused upon Your face.

When I look to You for what I should do
I'll be running an excellent race.

Then I'll gaze in Your eyes, having won first prize-
Of Your loving and warm embrace!
             Penny Mandeville

<u>Prayer</u>
"You follow Me." I hear that loud and clear, Lord. You are my Goal for everything in life. Thank you that Your indwelling Spirit leads me into all truth. I am never without direction, never without focus, never without Your fullness for all that lies ahead. Teach me. In Your amazing Name. Amen.

<u>Reflections</u>
1. My favorite "follow Jesus" passage is the gospel of John, chapter 10, the story of the Good Shepherd and the sheep. Read verses 1-30 and make note of the words and phrases that indicate what following Jesus means.

2. Record them in your journal. Talk to the Lord about what you discover.

42. Vertigo: Walking Wobbly in This World

…that you may be filled with the knowledge of his will
in all spiritual wisdom and understanding,
so as to walk in a manner worthy of the Lord,
fully pleasing to him: bearing fruit in every good work
Colossians 1:9-10 ESV

I'm walking wobbly these days. Intermittent vertigo and bouts of mild dizziness have been mine as I go about my daily life. They are difficult because I never know when it will hit. The two times while I was driving were terrifying.

So I've had to make changes. Testing determined that a couple of small, past strokes in the balance area of my brain are likely the cause of my symptoms. Scary but good to know and now to process.

Coming to grips with weakness and aging and mortality can produce a perspective that has been fine-tuned and deep and rich. And so this is happening afresh and anew for me. And I'm listening for the Voice of my indwelling Shepherd ever more closely.

> My sheep listen to my voice; I know them, and they follow me.   John 10:27 NLT

And I'm asking Him, "Are these the 'good things' You have for me to do at this stage of my life?"

> For we are God's masterpiece. He has created us anew in Christ Jesus, so we can do the good things he planned for us long ago.   Ephesians 2:10 NLT

And thankfully, I can "walk worthy," even while I "walk wobbly" in this world. My true stability is fixed. I am His and He is mine. I am in Him, my Rock, and He is in me, His dwelling place and His instrument in my wobbly world.

Can I ask you, my friend, "What is your wobble?" Is it . . .
> physical — chronic physical illnesses and handicap?
> emotional — anxiety, depression, loneliness?
> relational — loneliness, "excluded," separation, divorce, widowhood, estrangement?

No matter what it is, why not join me in "walking wobbly" and "walking worthy" in our Stable One — our indwelling Lord Jesus Christ by the power of the Spirit.

> And we believers also groan, even though we have the Holy Spirit within us as a foretaste of future glory, for we long for our bodies to be released from sin and suffering. We, too, wait with eager hope for the day when God will give us our full rights as his adopted children, including the new bodies he has promised us. We were given this hope when we were saved. Romans 8:23-24 NLT

> That is why we never give up. Though our bodies are dying, our spirits are being renewed every day. For our present troubles are small and won't last very long. Yet they produce for us a glory that vastly outweighs them and will last forever! So we don't look at the troubles we can see now; rather, we fix our gaze on things that cannot be seen. For the things we see now will soon be gone, but the things we cannot see will last forever.   2 Corinthians 4:16-18 NLT

<u>Aging with Grace</u>

I can feel my body aging
And I start to feel depressed.
Many new health problems
Each day bring a new test.

I can slump into depression
And give up the joy of youth.
Or sink into Your arms of love
And listen to Your truth!

You say with age comes wisdom
You give new mercies every day.
Through trials we learn endurance
When we trust You'll lead the way.

In acceptance there's contentment
When we acknowledge the life we're given
Through perseverance we find hope
For the adventure we are living.

You help us face the challenges
Of aging as we grow
In character and faithfulness
For deep within we know

That though our bodies are becoming
Less suitable for this earth
Our spirits and souls are being made whole
For our ultimate and final rebirth!
Penny Mandeville

<u>Prayer</u>
Lord God, our Rock and our Stability,
We walk in You today. We rest in You. We abide in You. We cling to You. We snuggle down deep in You today. Lead us in Your path for us, no matter how wobbly it may be. We trust You, our only Hope and Surety. In Jesus Name. Amen.

<u>Reflections</u>
1. Waking Words for Wobbly Ones:

> Today as you step into what may be a "wobbly day," look for this song on Youtube:
> "He Will Hold Me Fast" (Getty) and sing along as you begin your day.
> Here is the chorus:

> *He will hold me fast, He will hold me fast;*
> *For my Saviour loves me so, He will hold me fast.*[53]

2. Wondrous Words for Wobbly Ones:

> Today is a "first time," because each day brings new "adventures" in our worthy walk with our Lord. Today read Psalm 92 and observe:

> Even as "wobbly ones," we have so many reasons to be thankful (vs 1-2) and to be amazed at what our God does on our behalf (vs 4-6). His promise is that He will bring forth fruit in our wobbly, wounded lives to His glory and worthiness even into our old age (vs 12-15).
> Thank You, our Loving Lord!

3. Stability for a Worried Wobbler:

> We have an enemy who would love to grab hold of our mind and cause us to worry, fear, agonize over the "what if's" of our wobbliness. We are tempted to wear our worries and anxieties as a garment, forgetting … "BUT GOD."

> 1 Peter 5:6-11 is the perfect "go to" passage for times like these. Journal what the Holy Spirit says to your mind and heart. Be sure to notice what your attitude toward God is, what your action toward your enemy is, and what will be God's result?

43. The Wave: Abandoning to God

Jesus called loudly, "Father, I place my life in your hands!"
Luke 23:46 MSG

Several years ago in August we were at Bethany Beach, Delaware with our daughter and son-in-law and their three amazing boys. It was a hot one. No, a scorcher. Try a 96 degree one.
So we went on the beach early, and the two older boys jumped right in.

I'm a beach lover, and I love the ocean water. But I'm hardly a daredevil. So I enjoyed *vicariously* the freedom of the boys' fun as they jumped into the waves.

The thing that most struck me about all the beach fun was little Eli. He was actually "flinging" himself bodily into the waves, abandoning himself to the uncertainty and the scary thrill of the surf.

As I nervously awaited his appearance above each swallowing wave, I was amazed at the look on his little emerging face. First, a bit of sputtering but then sheer joy. Joy!

The Holy Spirit spoke to my heart in that very moment, "That's what abandonment will produce in you, Jan, as you fling yourself into Me…every moment of every day, no matter the waves and surf of your circumstances." As I meditated on this truth, the realization came to my mind that my abandonment to the Lord gives Him great joy also. Yes, Him.

Back to the beach with Eli. I couldn't help but feel the same thrilling joy as I watched his sweet little face fill with exhilaration. How could I not?

The Scripture says,

> …the joy of the Lord is your strength.
> Nehemiah 8:10

So the Lord's joy, the joy that He "feels," is what strengthens us for whatever we face, whatever wave comes our way. And His joyful Presence empowers us with Himself. After all, the fruit of the Spirit is joy. His joy.

And again, Jesus said that He has spoken His life-giving words…

> …so that you will be filled with my joy. Yes, your joy will overflow!
> John 15:10 NLT

I love the benediction at the end of the book of Jude:

> Now all glory to God, who is able to keep you from falling away and will bring you with great joy into his glorious presence without a single fault.
> All glory to him who alone is God, our Savior through Jesus Christ our Lord. All glory, majesty, power, and authority are his before all time, and in the present, and beyond all time! Amen.
> Jude 24-25 NLT

One day we children of God will each have great joy to go into our Father's Presence. But also Jesus Himself will be elated to usher us into His Father's Presence. Can you just picture His amazing face filled with indescribable joy as HE Himself walks us into the Throne room—we who have been kept by His power, faultless for that day? Amazing.

So brothers and sisters, *fling* yourself today into that indwelling Ocean of God and be filled with the Lord's own unfettered joy…your strength.

> Brothers and sisters … I urge you to offer your bodies as a living and holy sacrifice to God, a sacred offering that brings Him pleasure; this is your reasonable, essential worship.
> Romans 12:1 VOICE

<u>The Jump</u>
When at last I jump right in
I'm throwing caution to the wind.

But, No! It isn't to the wind
I'm throwing caution unto Him!

He alone makes all things new.
I'm trusting Him in all I do.

Others may not understand.
But I'll not stray from Jesus' plan.

No matter whom I might annoy
I only know with Him is JOY.

Joy that's with me all my days.
Joy that fills my heart with praise!
        Penny Mandeville

<u>Prayer</u>

O Lord of the Waves, I fling myself into You afresh today. Fill me with Your Joy. Empower me to face whatever comes my way today–You and me, joyfully together. In Your Name. Amen.

<u>Reflections</u>

1. If you are a swimmer, picture yourself "flinging yourself" into God the next time you are at a pool or beach. If you, like me, are not a swimmer, <u>visualize</u> throwing yourself into the Ocean that is God. You can wrap yourself in your favorite blanket (mine is a crocheted "ocean wave blanket"). Let yourself feel "submerged" in the Ocean of God Who is Love. Do you feel His joy welling up inside your soul? Thank Him and know that He also rejoices in your abandonment to Him.

2. Sing the hymn, *O the Deep, Deep Love of Jesus*. (Find it in a hymn book or on YouTube). Enjoy the ocean imagery:

> *O the deep, deep love of Jesus*
> *Vast unmeasured, boundless, free*
> *Rolling as a mighty ocean*
> *In its fullness over me ...*[54]

GLORY IN THE EMPTYING

You will never know the fullness of Christ until you know the emptiness of everything but Christ.[55]
Charles Spurgeon

44. The Nest: Emptying to be Filled

For in Christ all the fullness of the Deity lives in bodily form,
and in Christ you have been brought to fullness.
He is the head over every power and authority.
Colossians 2:9-10 NIV

There are lots of *emptyings* in life. There are deaths and losses of
every kind. There are ends of relationships, ends of jobs, ends of
school-years, ends of eras, ends of phases of life. Some of these are
expected. Some catch us by surprise.

Motherhood, in particular, is filled with *emptyings*—from the
emptying of the womb in childbirth to the emptying of self in child-
raising. The stripping is hard, every step along the way. And then
there is an *emptying* that affects all mothers sooner or later—the
emptying of the nest.

I know. This is what we have been preparing our children for, right?
The launch, the flight out of the safety, security, and nurturing of
their childhood home, out into the excitement of what God has for
them up ahead. But who prepares moms for this? Releasing my
children into adulthood, to make their own way, caught me by
surprise. It was harder than I ever thought.

My mind goes back to a Mothers' Day at the very start of this
emptying. The Lord in a unique way comforted my grieving
heart. It was at a time when my children, who were young adults,
had just gone through some serious health crises. So I was drained
emotionally.

At that time, there were "significant others" in the picture. So celebrating Mothers' Day became somewhat of a dilemma. Those "significant others' also had mothers. So we decided to postpone our celebration to the following Sunday. That should have taken care of it, right? But to my surprise, being alone on the *real* Mothers' Day was a grief to me.

I was struggling, trying not to wallow in my sadness, when the Lord surprised me with three gifts. Three delights for a hurting mama's heart. Three *God-winks* that most likely would have gone unnoticed had we been celebrating that day.

The first gift was finding old cassette tapes of my *babies'* voices. They had been packed away for years–precious tapes of Jeremy and Beth when each of them was just starting to talk; others, when they were very young. One was even labeled "doing school and being obnoxious." I listened...I laughed...I cried...as the bitter-sweetness of those precious voices washed over me.

The second *sacred wink* was catching sight of a mama house finch launching her babies. Talk about the perfect metaphor at the perfect time. The mama of the little family of house finches had nested in a bush next to our porch. She was giving this sorrowing mama a lesson in the *circle of life.* I imagined mama finch saying her good-byes as each left the safety of her nest. Was she grieving the way I was? Or was she more courageous than I?

And last but not least, I just "happened" to come across a monthly ministry letter from *Telling the Truth*. I had tossed it aside to join my stack of others to be read *someday*. But by God's grace, in that alone time, I picked it up and started reading. And then it all came together.

Stuart Briscoe, describing how motherhood had changed his wife Jill, wrote:

> When the baby was born, I stood by helplessly and watched the transformation that took place in my wife. Motherhood changed her irrevocably. As she nursed her child I detected a mysterious gleam in her eyes—a certain glow, a knowing, a secret insight that she shared with the new arrival. She and he knew something that I didn't know. I could do nothing more than observe and wonder at the mystery of motherhood.

Stuart went on to say...

> It occurs to me that the unique bond between mother and child makes possible an intimate nurturing relationship that men never know for they, by definition, are removed—they stand at a distance from the mother-child phenomenon. But hard as it can be for the father to make the adjustment to the beloved intruder, there is divine genius in the arrangement. For the day comes—all too soon—when the child must spread his wings and take flight from the nest. Guess who struggles at this point? The mother, of course! Releasing and relinquishing are not mother gifts. Guess who knows how to handle distance? The father, naturally. So as the wise mother has steered the puzzled father through the mysteries of nurturing, so the wise father now steps forward to guide the fearful mother through the anxieties of relinquishment. And the child receives what he needs—a healthy balance of mother nurture and father freedom...[56]

What a comfort these words were. Having never gone through this phase of life before, I was struggling. And as hard as it was and would continue to be for some time, it is God's way to move my children into responsible adulthood. It was their turn to step up to the plate of life and fulfill the will of God in their generation (Acts 13:36).

Emptyings are never easy...

So dear mama-sister, if you are going through *"the emptying of all emptyings"* (or so it seems at the time), open your eyes. There may be *God-winks* all around you, visitations from your Abba Father God to comfort a relinquishing mama's heart.

Don't Let Me Miss You
Every day has
Its share of disappointments.
When that is what I focus on
I miss Holy Spirit appointments!

I miss your subtle messages
You leave me everywhere.
I miss the gentle nudges
Which show how much you care!

Don't let me miss the blessings
You send along the way
Give me eyes to see your hand
Touching my life each day!
           Penny Mandeville

<u>Prayer</u>
Lord, I acknowledge that I am as full as I can ever be because I'm filled with You, dear Jesus. No matter what the emptying in this life, please remind me that I have all that I need in You. But open my eyes to Your "winks," Your gifts all around me. I don't want to grasp at anything in this life to fill my emptying. You are my all.

<u>Reflections</u>
1. What are the "emptyings" going on in your life? What are the disappointments that you are still holding onto?

2. Journal them, handing them over to the Lord, and ask Him how He may be filling you with new things.

45. The Empty House: Remembering Fullness

I came so that [you] would have life, and have it abundantly.
John 10:10 NASB (emphasis added)

I was never a fan of poetry. And even though I had amazing English teachers in high school, I hated studying "Poetry." None of it made sense to me — all those figures of speech, irregular word order, free verse, etc. Well, all of that has changed as I have grown older. Experiencing more of life has opened me up to truly appreciate poetry.

Recently, I was tutoring a Chinese teenager in English. So I decided to expose her to some good American poetry. And who better than Joyce Kilmer, an American poet, best known for his magnificent poem, "Trees."

Kilmer was a native of the area where I grew up—New Brunswick/Edison, New Jersey. I remember memorizing that poem with my fourth-grade classmates, enjoying its rhythm and rhyme. So I searched for poems by Kilmer. And eureka! I came across a gem that grabbed me deeply.

<u>The House with Nobody in It</u>
By Joyce Kilmer

Whenever I walk to Suffern along the Erie track
I go by a poor old farmhouse with its shingles broken and black.
I suppose I've passed it a hundred times, but I always stop for a minute
And look at the house, the tragic house, the house with nobody in it.

I never have seen a haunted house, but I hear there are such things;
That they hold the talk of spirits, their mirth and sorrowings.

I know this house isn't haunted, and I wish it were, I do;
For it wouldn't be so lonely if it had a ghost or two.

This house on the road to Suffern needs a dozen panes of glass,
And somebody ought to weed the walk and take a scythe to the grass.
It needs new paint and shingles, and the vines should be trimmed and
        tied;
But what it needs the most of all is some people living inside.

If I had a lot of money and all my debts were paid
I'd put a gang of men to work with brush and saw and spade.
I'd buy that place and fix it up the way it used to be
And I'd find some people who wanted a home and give it to them free.

Now, a new house standing empty, with staring window and door,
Looks idle, perhaps, and foolish, like a hat on its block in the store.
But there's nothing mournful about it; it cannot be sad and lone
For the lack of something within it that it has never known.

But a house that has done what a house should do, a house that has
        sheltered life,
That has put its loving wooden arms around a man and his wife,
A house that has echoed a baby's laugh and held up his stumbling feet,
Is the saddest sight, when it's left alone, that ever your eyes could meet.

So whenever I go to Suffern along the Erie track
I never go by the empty house without stopping and looking back,
Yet it hurts me to look at the crumbling roof and the shutters fallen apart,
For I can't help thinking the poor old house is a house with a broken
        heart.[58]

When I first read this poem and for many readings thereafter, I
would find myself almost sobbing with grief…over a house…an
empty house…a house with no one, no person in it. The
personification had overwhelmed me with its sadness. And even
with the passage of time, I couldn't get the imagery out of my mind
— a poor, lonely, empty home.

But the message began to go even deeper, as I've observed empty, lonely people—people who are like Kilmer's house. They were like empty "mobile homes," moving their way through the craziness of this world without life and love and direction and stability and purpose and hope.

And as I reflected, I remembered Jesus—Jesus who gives people life—abundant, over the top life. He comes to live His matchless, full life within people, His dwelling places.

> "Look! I stand at the door and knock. If you hear my voice and open the door, I will come in, and we will share a meal together as friends." Revelation 3:20 NLT

> Don't you realize that your body is the temple of the Holy Spirit, who lives in you and was given to you by God?
> 1 Corinthians 6:19 NLT

So now what deeply moves me is an amazing truth. Little ole, formerly empty and lonely me is no longer empty and barren. I'm no longer without life and hope. Now in Christ, I am the dwelling place of the living God by the Holy Spirit. I am never alone and empty — I'm filled with the fullness of God.

And this is true of you, dear sister and brother in Christ. You are no longer empty and desolate. You are filled with the fullness of Life, our Lord Jesus Christ. Let's thank and praise Him.

The Empty House
A vacant shell
A dried up well
A barn with an empty stall

A rainless cloud
A field unplowed
A school with no children at all.

They each lack the presence
Of the very essence
That brings meaning to their existence.

It's the same in our hearts
Until Jesus imparts His new life
And we give no resistance.
                Penny Mandeville

<u>Prayer</u>
O Living Lord, Filler of emptiness. Thank You that I am never desolate. I am never abandoned. You are in me in all Your fullness. Cause me to remember Your indwelling Presence wherever I go and whatever I face today. You are with me and for me and in me. Thank you.
And lead me to someone today who is empty, lonely, longing to receive from You. May I be the expresser of Your life and love to them. In Your Full Name. Amen.

<u>Reflections</u>
1. What were your thoughts and impressions when you first read "The House with Nobody in It"? Can you apply it to your life, your own spiritual condition? Journal your own thoughts and personal application.

2. Spend some time with this thought today: we are passing sad, empty people every day. Ask the Lord to open your eyes today to

those around you, so you can express the fullness of Christ in your world:

- Is there a prayer you can pray for the clerk at the store?
- Is there a door you can open for a struggling mom?
- Is there a smile and hello for that older person who looks sad and lonely?
- Is there a word from Jesus you can share with a spiritually hungry soul?
- Is there a ___________________? You get the idea.

46. The Delay: Embracing God's Plan A

Now Jesus <u>loved </u>Martha and her sister and Lazarus.
<u>So </u>when He heard that he was sick,
He then stayed two days longer in the place where He was.
John 11:5 NASB, emphasis mine

Did you ever have your "neat and tidy plans" totally turned upside down because of a major delay beyond your control? That was the situation when our daughter Beth had an unexpected C-section while giving birth to our grandson William. Our carefully laid plans to be there to help were lengthened, and Plan A was blown apart.

As I contemplated the changes in our plans, I was simultaneously studying John 11. I couldn't help but see the major changes Jesus and his friends were about to experience.

> Now a certain man was sick, Lazarus of Bethany, the village of Mary and her sister Martha... So the sisters sent word to Him, saying, "Lord, behold, he whom You love is sick." But when Jesus heard this, He said, "This sickness is not to end in death, but for the glory of God, so that the Son of God may be glorified by it." Now Jesus <u>loved </u>Martha and her sister and Lazarus. <u>So</u> when He heard that he was sick, He then stayed two days longer in the place where He was.
> John 11:1-5 NASB (emphasis added)

Now that makes no sense at all, does it? When Jesus heard about the sickness of His friend, He delayed...He waited...and Mary and Martha and Lazarus waited too. In fact, Jesus caused them to wait.

Why? Because of love...yes, love. Did you notice that?

He loved Mary...and He loved Martha...and
He loved Lazarus. So He stayed…

"So" is such a significant word. He loved each of them, *so* He delayed. And because of that significant delay, each of them experienced something unique with their friend and Lord.

Martha, who is the "mover and shaker" of the group, received deep theological truth for her heart as well as her mind. And she would soon see this truth played out in action in a Person.

> Jesus said to her, "I am the resurrection and the life; he who believes in Me will live even if he dies, and everyone who lives and believes in Me will never die. Do you believe this?" She said to Him, "Yes, Lord; I have believed that You are the Christ, the Son of God, even He who comes into the world." John 11:25-27 NASB

Mary, the tenderhearted mystic, experienced the empathy of Her Lord and Savior in the midst of her grief. The Son of God wept with her.

> When Jesus therefore saw her weeping, and the Jews who came with her also weeping, He was deeply moved in spirit and was troubled, and said, "Where have you laid him?" They said to Him, "Lord, come and see." Jesus wept. John 11:33-35 NASB

And then Lazarus, the beloved brother, experienced not just a healing of an illness, like many others had experienced at the hand of the Savior, but life from the dead. Resurrection!

Jesus said, "Remove the stone"…So they removed the
stone…He cried out with a loud voice, "Lazarus, come
forth." The man who had died came forth…
John 11:38-44 NASB

Wow.

So here is the truth I saw about our waiting in Delaware. God loves
me and He loves each of my loved ones. So He delays, because He
knows what He is about in each of our lives. So His Plan A is often
our Plan B or C or not our plan at all.

And I realized by God's grace that if I had a bad attitude in it all, I
would miss experiencing the Lord in His own unique way for my
life. Furthermore, if I tried to rescue my loved ones (husband,
children, grandsons...), if I tried to save them from difficulty and
disappointment, if I tried to make them okay, I could be standing in
God's way in their lives. His delay is purposeful in each of our
lives, uniquely and individually, just as it was with Mary and Martha
and Lazarus.

So it is for you too, my friend. What are you going through right
now? Are you being kept waiting in a health crisis, family
upheaval, frustrated dreams and ambitions?

Just know this, struggling one. He loves you, *so* He is
waiting. Don't miss Him. Rest in Him. He will surprise you with
His peace. And you will experience who He is, in and through what
you are going through right now.

PS. I'm so glad I didn't miss the Lord in Delaware. As it turned out,
those extra weeks were precious for relationships and the older boys

were able to go back to Ohio with us. Because of the Lord's delay, cousins could be together for a birthday. This wouldn't have been possible if our plan A had worked. God even cares about the "little ones." Thank you, Jesus. His Plan A is best.

<u>Waiting</u>
Waiting is the hardest thing
When you're searching for direction.
If I do this or if I do that
Would You have any objection?

I'm willing to do either
If you'll just show me Your will.
I'm trying to be patient
But it's hard to just sit still.

But maybe sitting still
Is exactly what I need.
Perhaps I'll grow when things are slow
Till You say how to proceed.

So help me, Lord, to hear Your voice
And may I not debate!
But trust You have a reason
When You're telling me to wait!
   Penny Mandeville

<u>Prayer</u>
Loving Lord, thank You that Your Plan A is always better than ours. Teach us to wait in faith and trust when we encounter Your delays. You know how hard it is for us to "play the waiting game,"

especially in times of trial. Teach us. Remind us by Your Holy Spirit who indwells us. In Your Patient Name. Amen.

<u>Reflections</u>
1. Put yourself and your loved ones in the John chapter 11 story. What are the circumstances you and/or loved ones are facing right now? Are you playing the "waiting game"?

2. Put yourself and then each of your loved ones into this sentence:

Jesus loved ___________________, *so* He waited

___________________________.

What is He waiting to do in your life? Your loved one's life?
Has He revealed any *Why*'s?
Do you sense His presence with you and your loved one in it all?
Is He speaking truth to you or your loved one, like Martha?
Is He crying with you, like Mary?
Is He doing something extraordinary, as with Lazarus?

3. Journal your meditation.

47. Dust to Glory: Honoring a Sanctuary

...for you are dust,
and to dust you shall return.
Genesis 3:19 ESV

These words, spoken every Ash Wednesday in many Christian churches, has taken on a new meaning for me since my 91 year old mom passed away. Something arrested me the day of my mom's funeral. Maybe it started with the incense and the reverence afforded the treatment of my dear mama's frail little body being put to rest. I was undone by deep sobs of realization.

It wasn't the finality of it all. It had already been final when she had breathed her last, days before. No. It was the "sacredness" that came crashing through.

> *My mama's feeble and now even ashen body had been the very dwelling place of GOD!*

And that sacredness started long before her death. The sacredness was about the Glory, the Living God Himself, indwelling that humble little person, Jeanette Galuszka Renner—day after day, year after year of her joyful, suffering life.

The gilded family Bible sitting on our coffee table had declared it everywhere:

> "Or do you not know that your body is a temple [a Holy of Holies] of the Holy Spirit within you, whom you have from God?"   1 Corinthians 6:19 NASB

"Christ in you, the hope of glory." Colossians 1:27 NASB
"...the Spirit of God dwells in you." Romans 8:9 NASB
"But we have this treasure [the glorious Christ] in jars of
clay [our bodies], to show that the surpassing power belongs
to God and not to us."
2 Corinthians 4:7 NASB (emphasis added)

And on and on. In fact, it proved true her favorite verse that she had
often quoted to me as a child:

"What no eye has seen, nor ear heard, nor the heart of man
imagined, what God has prepared for those who love him…"

And then is added...

"…these things God has revealed to us through the Spirit." 1
Corinthians 2:9-10 ESV

A friend named Don had tried to tell me this very truth not long
before he went home to Jesus. Though his body had been decaying,
Don knew that Jesus was living in that falling apart "dwelling." And
he wanted me to write about it.

I had another friend, young but soon "going home." Her "divine
dwelling place" was getting more and more misshapen and failing.
Oh, but the glory! There was no doubt when you entered her room,
you entered a sacred place where God lived.

All of them, and we too who know our Lord, are "sacred places,"
Holies of Holies of the Living God. And the Glory is there, because
He is there. It doesn't matter how frail, broken, misshapen we think

we may be. We are each a perfect home for God Himself on this earth, despite our "dustiness."

And that's not all -- soon very soon, glory forever.

> So we do not lose heart. Though our outer self is wasting away, our inner self is being renewed day by day. For this light momentary affliction is preparing for us an eternal weight of glory beyond all comparison, as we look not to the things that are seen but to the things that are unseen. For the things that are seen are transient, but the things that are unseen are eternal.
> 2 Corinthians 4:16-18 ESV

The Echo of Hymns

The old country church was abandoned, forgotten
Stained glass windows broken, wooden door rotting.

But inside there's an echo of hymns that were sung,
Prayers that were prayed and renewed lives begun.

For it once was a place people went to pursue Him
There's a hint of His presence, though the structure's in ruin.

It's the same with our bodies when we breathe our last breath.
There's a dignity that remains even after our death.

For our bodies, no matter how crippled or frail,
Hold the Spirit of the One who once tore the veil.

For He conquered all sickness and death when He rose
And He's lived deep within us, for that's what He chose.

And He Who's so loving and gracious to forgive us
Will accompany us Home to spend eternity with us.
          Penny Mandeville

<u>Prayer</u>
Glorious Lord God, what a privilege to be Your dwelling place on this earth. Thank you for brothers and sisters who have reflected Your Glory in the midst of their dustiness. May we show forth who You are even in our frail and fading humanity. In Jesus' Everlasting Name. Amen.

<u>Reflections</u>
1. Make a list of those who have already gone home to Jesus. How did they each show forth the glory of God in their "dustiness"?

2. Make a list of loved ones, friends, others who are showing forth the glory of God in the midst of their frailty, handicap, sickness, declining years. How do you see the Lord in them?

3. Reflect. Talk to the Lord about the lists. Thank the Lord for faithful witnesses, past and present. Pray for those still alive. Talk to the Lord about your thoughts. Journal.

48. The Mystery: Knowing Christ in You

…the riches of the glory of this mystery
…which is Christ in you, the hope of glory.
Colossians 1:27 NASB

Everyone loves a good mystery. Our family got hooked years ago on Sherlock Holmes, Hercule Poirot, *Murder She Wrote*, Miss Marple, etc. I guess the pleasure in mysteries is that the viewer is always trying to figure out "who done it." With lots of practice, I developed a pretty good track record. I love the challenge of putting the clues together.

God has mysteries too. But His mysteries are very different than the ones we try to figure out. Without His revelation, we could never know His mysteries. They are totally beyond our mental capabilities. We must depend on God to reveal them to us. Many of His mysteries God has revealed in Scripture.

But counterfeit spiritual mysteries abound everywhere, thanks to God's chief counterfeiter, the devil. Take, for instance, the one I encountered one day several years ago. I was checking out at a favorite bookstore, when a counter display caught my eye. The display was advertising a best seller, *The Secret* by Rhonda Byrne. This book explores the "Law of Attraction"—a cosmic theory, stating our thoughts determine our destiny.

Immediately the thought came to me, "I know the secret…it's Christ in me." And this *secret* (a.k.a. *mystery*) is no cosmic theory. It is a cosmic fact of monumental proportions. Paul, under the inspiration of the Holy Spirit, had disclosed it to believers of the first century and so to believers down through the ages. He describes it as "the mystery which has been hidden from the past ages and generations, but has now been manifested to His saints…the riches of the glory of this mystery…which is *Christ in you*, the hope of glory" Colossians 1:26, 27 NASB (emphasis added).

What a treasure of a truth. The living Lord Jesus Christ, the Son of God, second person of the Trinity, resides in you and in me who belong to him by faith. And according to the Scriptures, this is at the heart of a definition of a Christian in Scripture. Paul, in his letter to the Corinthians, exhorts the believers (and us):

> Test yourselves to see if you are in the faith, examine yourselves. Or do you not recognize this about yourselves, that Jesus Christ is in you—unless indeed you fail the test. 2 Corinthians 13:5 NASB

Christ in you is a mystery no longer. But can we fully fathom it even now? Not really. But it has been revealed to us by God. It would seem that many of us go for years without embracing this glorious truth. We live like *Christ in you* is still an unrevealed mystery. Some of us may even go to heaven not knowing and living it. How sad. The devil's lie he feeds to believers constantly is we are separate from our God. So now we need to do the best we can to live the Christian life.

We tend to live from our brains, our know-how, our emotions. We follow the Christian to-do lists that are given to us by others through books, talks, blogs, Facebook, sermons, etc. What we need is a fresh illumination by the Holy Spirit to really grasp the truth of *Christ in us* on the deepest of levels.

Christ lives his life in and through us as we depend on him.

I love how Dr. Wayne Barber says it. He imagines the conversation between the desperate believer and his indwelling Lord this way:

> Believer: "I can't."
>   Lord: "I never said you could."
> Believer: "You can."
>   Lord: "I always said I would."[58]

What about you, dear child of God? Have you had that inner illumination by the Holy Spirit of the indwelling Christ? Christ is in you. He's your only hope of experiencing the glory of God in and through your life.

Focus on *Him* living in you.

> He's on the throne at the right hand of the Father in heaven.
> He's nearby in the circumstances of your life.
> You're in him along with all your brothers and sisters in Christ.
> But right NOW and always, HE IS IN YOU.
> Focus on Him IN you.

<u>The Mystery</u>
I have a Holy Treasure
Deep inside of me.

The power, wisdom and love of God
It is a mystery.

The Maker of the universe,
How could it possibly be?

That He would send His Holy Spirit
To live inside of me?

He comforts me, He counsels me,
And I'm so thankful to be

A child of God with His Spirit inside
A burdened soul set free!
                    Penny Mandeville

<u>Prayer</u>
Lord Jesus, it is so easy for me to think of You as separate from me—out there somewhere.
But You are in ME. Thank You for the Holy Spirit who makes this possible. The same LORD Jesus Christ, seated on the throne at the right hand of the Father, is the Person living in MY spirit by YOUR Holy Spirit. May this truth sink deep into my mind and heart. In Your Name. Amen.

<u>Reflections</u>
1. Spend some time reflecting on the following beautiful Scriptures. Read each one thoughtfully and prayerfully. Write them in your journal. Surrender to your Teacher, the Holy Spirit, to reveal the indwelling Christ to your heart.

    Colossians 1:27–29
    2 Corinthians 4:6–7
    Galatians 2:20
    John 17:20–23
    1 John 4:4
    2 Corinthians 13:5
    Ephesians 3:14–21

2. Yield by faith to the Lord Jesus Christ to live his life in and through you today. Journal your thoughts and prayers

GLORY IN THE FIGHT

The devil and his demons are bullies.
But in the presence of Christ, they become wimps.[59]
Pete Briscoe

49. The Bully: Resisting in Faith

Submit yourselves therefore to God.
Resist the devil, and he will flee from you.
James 4:7 ESV

I love the old Westerns. Whenever I am home in the afternoon and have some time to relax, I turn on Me-TV and enjoy *Gunsmoke* or *The Rifleman* or *Rawhide*.

What is it about these shows? They take me back to my childhood. And they speak of a simpler time when right was right and wrong was wrong. But more than all that, the good guys always win.

Often there's a scenario where the poor dirt farmer in the story gets bullied by some heartless, powerful, rich rancher. It's usually to get him to sell his land at some ridiculous price—for the water rights or the railroad access. But eventually, and often not till the end of the story, the "good guy" rescues the underdog by standing up to the bully and overcoming him. The bully then wimps out or is destroyed.

I love that.

And don't we all love that in real life?

Well, as believers and lovers of our Lord Jesus Christ, we have a bully, the bully of all bullies. He is God's arch-enemy and therefore, ours -- Satan and his forces. And I remember a time the bully totally caught me off-guard.

I was at a three-day conference, doing a workshop and selling my books to homeschoolers. I came into the conference already tired from several months of an already packed schedule. From the very start, there seemed to be a "gray cloud" hanging over the entire thing for me (so unlike the previous year).

Thoughts like, "I can't do this."

"If I could just pack right up and go home, I would."

"I don't even know what to say about my book."

"This is too hard to be talking to people all day, day after day,"

All these negatives flooded my mind. So discouragement, pessimism, doubt, even blankness toward the presence of the Holy Spirit grabbed hold of my soul.

Finally, by the end of the second day, I began to ask the Lord about it. Was there something He was trying to tell me? Am I "done" in some way?

That's when the still small Voice of the Spirit broke through with one word, "Opposition."

Opposition? Really?

Yes. Spiritual Opposition.

Of course. And I hadn't recognized it. The bully was doing a good job of bullying me. But then the solution also came, "Resist. Stand firm in the Lord and in the strength of His might."

So I said a resounding, "No, I'm standing in my Christ." The bully wimped away in the Presence of my Lord, the King, the Conqueror, the ultimate "Good Guy." The gray clouds gradually began to lift. And the glorious Peace of Christ reigned.

I hadn't realized that the darkness, the depletion, the discouragement didn't come from myself unaided. They had been nudged along by the bully powers of darkness on my exhausted soul and body. And I had caved.

But now in the manifest Presence of my Lord, I could walk into my day in light, rather than darkness, clarity instead of confusion. I was still exhausted and even had to sit for half of the day. But the heaviness had lifted. Even though my circumstances hadn't changed, my heart attitude had.

Dear brothers & sisters, are you experiencing darkness, discouragement, confusion, condemnation, lethargy? Don't be ignorant of the bully's schemes as I was. It's an admonition easy to forget. He will come at us with all kinds of tactics when we are most vulnerable–in times of exhaustion, relational conflict, failures, disappointment.

> Humble yourselves, therefore, under the mighty hand of God so that at the proper time he may exalt you, casting all your anxieties on him, because he cares for you.
> Be sober-minded; be watchful. Your adversary the devil prowls around like a roaring lion, seeking someone to

devour. <u>Resist him, firm in your faith</u>, knowing that the same kinds of suffering are being experienced by your brotherhood throughout the world.
And after you have suffered a little while, the God of all grace, who has called you to his eternal glory in Christ, will himself restore, confirm, strengthen, and establish you.
To him be the dominion forever and ever. Amen.
1 Peter 5:6-10 ESV (emphasis added)

Finally, <u>be strong in the Lord and in the strength of his might</u>. Put on the whole armor of God, that you may be able to <u>stand</u> against the schemes of the devil. For we do not wrestle against flesh and blood, but against the rulers, against the authorities, against the cosmic powers over this present darkness, against the spiritual forces of evil in the heavenly places. Therefore take up the whole armor of God [which is Jesus Himself], that you may be able to withstand in the evil day, and having done all, to stand firm. Stand therefore, having fastened on the belt of truth, and having put on the breastplate of righteousness, and, as shoes for your feet, having put on the readiness given by the gospel of peace. In all circumstances take up the shield of faith, with which you can extinguish all the flaming darts of the evil one; and take the helmet of salvation, and the sword of the Spirit, which is the word of God.
Ephesians 6:10-17 ESV (emphasis added)

Remember, the bully has his schemes. But don't be his next victim. Consider yourself dead to his tactics, because you are. And you are alive in the Conquering King.

So resist, stand, and watch him wimp away in the presence of your indwelling Hero.

<u>Recognize the Voice</u>
There's a bully in my life
Who tries to discourage me.

He heaps great condemnation
And I'm down as I can be.

But then I recognize the voice
Is the voice of the enemy.

Those thoughts were not my thoughts at all
That gave me anxiety.

In Your strength I can resist him
And the enemy must flee.

I can cast my cares upon You, Lord,
Because You care for me!
           Penny Mandeville

<u>Prayer</u>
Lord Jesus, You are my conquering Hero. Why does it take me so long to recognize attacks by the bully of my soul? Remind me to resist and take my stand in You, my Strong One. Now and forever. In Your bully-shattering Name. Amen.

<u>Reflections</u>

1. When does the bully seem to trap you? What are the circumstances that make you most vulnerable? Check out the list above. Can you identify?

2. Meditate on the passages above. What are the Lord's exhortations in each? Journal the thoughts the Lord highlights to your mind and heart.

50. The Web: Getting Free

"I will remember their sins and their lawless deeds no more."
Where there is forgiveness of these,
there is no longer any offering for sin.
Hebrews 10:17-18 ESV

Early one morning my friend Penny and I were walking down a little-traveled path in my neighborhood. We were stopped dead in our tracks. A perfectly formed circular spider web was hanging across the path, suspended by a thread. Here was one spider who was serious. She was ready to get a good catch that day.

Years before, a period of insecurity plagued my life. I became a good catch in a craftily constructed web—not made by earthly designs but that of the father of lies (John 8:44). It started out with a series of real, and perhaps imagined, rejections which then developed into a lie. It wouldn't have been so bad if I had recognized it for what it was. But I didn't. And so I embraced it as truth and struggled for many years.

Believing the lie caused me much emotional pain, fear, and confusion. It influenced my behavior. And it even started to poison other relationships and areas of my life. Finally, by the time I recognized it as a lie, I was so bound up in it that I couldn't get free.

I prayed. I cried. I tried to act against it. I attempted the positive mental mind games. I asked my praying friends to pray. I asked my husband to pray. All in vain. Until one day, I was reading and meditating in the little book of Colossians, preparing to teach it for the third time.

I read,

> [Since] you have been raised with Christ, keep seeking the things above, where Christ is, seated at the right hand of God…For you have died, and your life is hidden with Christ in God.   Colossians 3:1, 3 NASB

All of a sudden, the Spirit of God brought the lie to my mind, and with it came this realization:

> *Wait a minute! I died to that lie!*

That very moment, the power of the lie was broken in my experience. Here I had been begging and pleading for the Lord to do something He had already done through the Cross of Christ and my union with him. But I had not recognized it by faith in this situation. Once I did, everything changed. I was set free from the fear, confusion, and the agonizing emotions the lie had produced.

You may ask me how I knew that this was true. I remembered a little scriptural word *with* (*Greek = united with*) and the truths in the Scriptures.

> When Christ died, I died "united with" him.
> When Christ was buried, I was buried "united with" him.
> When Christ was raised, I was raised "united with" him to newness of life.

And what did I die to?

I died to sin (Rom. 6:3–14; Eph. 2:1–7; 2 Cor. 5:21; Col. 2:13).

I died to self, the "old man" (Rom. 6:6; 2 Cor. 5:17; Gal. 2:20; Col. 3:9–10).

I died to the flesh (Rom. 6:2, 6, 11; Gal. 5:24).

I died to the world (Col. 2:8; Gal. 6:14).

I died to the Law, to-do list religion (Rom. 7:4, 6; Gal. 3:13, 24–25).

I died to the deception and accusations of Satan (Col. 2:15; Heb. 2:14–15; 1 Peter 5:8; Rev. 12:9-10; 20:3, 8).

So now when that nasty lie and other accusations and condemnations rear their ugly heads, I say,

Wait a minute! I died to that!

And I'm alive, united with my risen Savior—adequate in and through Him to be what He has made me to be in this situation.

New Life

To the ways of the world
I have died with Christ.
To all the temptations
I'm no longer enticed.

For the life I now live
Christ is living through me.
And the life I once led
Means nothing to me.

I seek only His face

And desire only His will.
I was raised to a life
He will help me fulfill.
       Penny Mandeville

<u>Prayer</u>
Lord, You are my Deliverer, my Rescuer. Through my union with You in death and resurrection, I can live each day in victory over the world, the flesh, and the devil. Remind me, by Your Holy Spirit, to count on this to be true in my life today and every day. In your Powerful Name. Amen.

<u>Reflections</u>
1. What *lies, accusations, expectations,* and *condemnations* are you struggling with today?
What *besetting sin* has a grip on you? What *selfish desires* and *self-focus* harass your soul?

2. Look at the verses above that connect to your own struggle. Write out the verses in your journal. Read and meditate on the truth that sets you free:

> *On the basis of the Word of God, I say to you, you died to all of that. And now you are raised to walk in newness of life because of the One to Whom you are united in his resurrection fullness.*

3. Journal your own reflections and prayer. Remember,

> Your old life is dead. Your new life, which is your real life—even though invisible to spectators—is with Christ in God.

He is your life. When Christ (your real life, remember) shows up again on this earth, you'll show up, too—the real you, the glorious you.
Colossians 3:3–4 MSG

51. Planes and Boats and Prayer, O My! Inviting Jesus In

They were willing therefore to receive him into the boat...
John 6:21 ASV

It was late summer. I was preparing for a new school year with my new bunch of preschoolers at Xenia Christian. I was also going to meetings and doing home visits as a homeschool coordinator with the Dayton Christian Home School Program. As any teacher knows, mid-August, with its meetings and classroom prep, can get pretty hairy.

It was during this time that I received a call from my sister Nancy. She informed me that her husband Ed, who had been battling cancer, suddenly and surprisingly took a turn for the worse. He was now on life support, but there was little, if any, hope. Plans had been made to terminate life support at the end of the week. So I knew it meant a trip to New Jersey for a funeral.

I was totally stressed. In the midst of everything else that was going on, now a flight back East. I'm ashamed to admit this. But the thing that was stressing me the most by then was the thought of a plane flight.

I know, shame on me. My poor sister. And here I am freaking out about getting on a plane. I begged and pleaded with my husband to drive me to New Jersey, but he insisted, "There's no time! You've got to fly."

So on my way to a meeting that day, I agonized. All of a sudden, in the midst of my churning thoughts, the still, small Voice broke through:

Jesus walks with us on the chaos of our lives.

I recognized this as a line from the Oswald Chambers devotional I had been reading for years. I sensed it was significant, a word from the Lord. So I decided to find that familiar story when I got home. I knew that there would be a message from the Lord tucked away in that scripture.

So I pulled out my *Harmony of the Gospels,*[60] an old Bible study book with gospel accounts side-by-side chronologically. And as usual, I was not disappointed. I read all the details of the familiar story of Jesus walking on the water toward his terrified, struggling disciples.

Something I saw there absolutely shocked me. I had never noticed it before, as familiar as this story was.

Take a look with me:

> When it was evening, the boat was in the middle of the sea, and He was alone on the land. Seeing them straining at the oars, for the wind was against them, at about the fourth watch of the night He came to them, walking on the sea; and <u>He intended to pass by them.</u>

Wait a minute. What does it mean: "he intended to pass by them"? I had never noticed that before. Why would He do that? God doesn't play games. Why would He walk past? And would He really walk past, seeing his terrified, struggling disciples? Wasn't that why He was walking out to them in the first place? Or was it?

I decided to read on. I knew the answer must be there somewhere.

> But when they saw Him walking on the sea, they supposed that it was a ghost, and cried out; for they all saw Him and were terrified…But immediately He spoke with them and said to them, "Take courage; it is I, do not be afraid."
>
> <u>They were willing therefore to receive Him into the boat</u>…

Again, the Holy Spirit's sacred *highlighter*, so to speak. There it was. The Lord Jesus wanted to be invited. (Later I did a word study on this word *willing*. It means a volitional, intentional choice).

So I imagined that his struggling disciples, recognizing who Jesus was and what He could do, were more than willing. They were desperate to invite Him into their boat. And of course, we know what happened next:

> Then He got into the boat with them, and the wind stopped; and they were utterly astonished…And those who were in the boat worshiped him, saying, "You are certainly God's Son"…and immediately the boat was at the land to which they were going.
> Mark 6:47-51; Matthew 14:33; John 6:21 NASB (emphasis added)

Jesus can do that kind of thing because *He is certainly God's Son—* Sovereign, Almighty God in the flesh.

So you may have guessed what happened. That's right, I began to invite Him into *"my boat,"* every aspect of my stressful situation— into the purchase of the plane ticket, into the plane—the cockpit, cabin, under the wings, in the engine (Hey, I was desperate).

Then when we were in flight, it's as if I could see the Lord walking up and down the aisle, ministering to the other passengers too. The perfect Pilot as well as the perfect flight Attendant.

So I arrived at Newark airport without an ounce of anxiety, thanks to my amazing traveling Companion. And the same was true when I flew home.

When I arrived home, I was basking in the glow of it all. So I asked the Lord, "What just happened? What does it all mean?"

Then the simple truth dawned upon me…

Jesus wants me to invite Him into "my boat"—my specific life situation, whatever that may be.

This is prayer.

Let me ask you, dear friend: what is the *boat* you are in right now? Is it an unhealthy body, emotional upheaval, financial needs, unemployment, the daily-ness of raising children, spiritual struggles, anxiety attacks, shame, wayward children, confusion, facing a scary situation like a plane ride or speaking in public?

Whatever it may be, invite the Lord into "your boat."

Watch what He can do, because He is certainly God's Son.

The Invitation
Whenever you're in a situation
Of feeling shaken and remote
Offer to Jesus an invitation
To come into your boat.

He's always willing
To make tempest waves calm.
And quiets your soul
Like a soothing balm.
            Penny Mandeville

Prayer
Lord Jesus, I invite You into my "my boat," this situation I'm facing right now ______________.
I trust You to do what only You can. I am watching and waiting in faith for You to manifest Yourself in my situation. Thank you. Amen.

<u>Reflections</u>

1. Place a small plastic boat in a prominent place in your home or workplace to remind you to invite the Lord into the situations you face each day.

2. Look up this story in a good children's Bible story book and share what you have learned with a child in your life. Give them a boat also to remind them to invite Jesus into the situations they face in their young life.

3. Look at Luke 24:13-30 and Revelation 3:15-20. What are the circumstances, the invitation, and the response? Put yourself in each of the stories and invite Him in.

52. Last Words: Hearing the Words of Christ

Father, forgive them,
for they do not know what they are doing.
Luke 23:34 NASB

The last words of a dying person are significant. They are so final and so revealing of what is uppermost in a person's mind as he is leaving this earth to face his Maker.

I have been with several dying persons just shortly before their deaths. My grandmother died an untimely death. She had been hospitalized after a heart attack, but wasn't expected to die. But she did die, just before being released. I had visited her from out of town just days before.

I remember her looking at a picture of Christ hanging on the wall of her room and saying, "O how much he suffered for us." To me, these were her last words, reflecting a lifetime of devotion to her Lord.

Another person I visited shortly before his death was the father of a young friend. As I took his hand to pray for him that night in hospice, this dad struggled to say something. Finally, his words came: "I'm concerned about Mary's [not her real name] relationship with Jesus." I told Mary the next day about her dad's concern. That day she had time alone with him and said, "Daddy, I love Jesus." And right then her daddy went home to his Lord.

So last words can have an incredible impact on one's life. This is especially true of the last statements of our Savior from the cross. When we realize the agonizing physical death caused by crucifixion, it's incredible to think that our Lord would say what he said, hanging on a cruel cross. Angry, blaspheming words like those spoken by the criminals crucified with him would more readily come to mind for most people.

Christ spoke these statements as He was hanging on the cross, dying for you and for me.

> A word of forgiveness: "Father, forgive them for they do not know what they are doing." Luke 23:34 NIV
>
> A word of salvation: "I tell you the truth, today you will be with me in paradise." Luke 23:43 NCV
>
> A word of family affection: "Dear woman, here is your son . . . Here is your mother." John 19:26–27 NCV
>
> A word of abandonment: "My God, my God, why have you forsaken me?" Matthew 27:46 NIV
>
> A word of personal need: "I am thirsty." John 19:28 NIV
>
> A word of completion: "It is finished." John 19:30 NIV
>
> A word of reunion: "Father, into your hands I commit my spirit." Luke 23:46 NIV

Each of our Savior's words spoke love, hope, and truth to the people surrounding Him. He speaks those same words of love, hope, and truth to us today. Since our Savior lives His life through us, we can speak those life-giving words to others in our life.

Last Words

What will be the thoughts I'll think
Just before I die?
What will be the words I'll speak
To those who are nearby?

Will I be forgiving
Of those who've caused me pain?
Will I be concerned about
My loved ones who'll remain?

Will I anxiously be waiting
For You to come for me?
Or will this world have ties on me
And prevent my being free?

Lord, let me be ready
Before that day arrives
To make my peace with everyone
Who's come into my life.

Show me how to shed regret
For the things I shouldn't have done.
Instead, may I be thankful
For the things I've overcome.

Then, when it's time to go with You
My heart will be at peace.
And I can bless my loved ones
And into Your arms joyfully be released.
      Penny Mandeville

<u>Prayer</u>

Lord and Savior, Jesus Christ, I bow in awe of You and Your
selfless love for me. I am filled with gratitude for the new life that is
mine because of Your forgiving sacrifice on the cross. Thank You
for those precious words that captivate my mind and heart and life.

May I speak Your words of life and grace to those around me. In Your Loving Name. Amen.

<u>Reflections</u>

1. Visualize yourself right there beneath his cross:
Take in the sights, sounds, emotions, but above all, the words.
Receive them as your own.

2. Meditate on Jesus' sayings from the Cross, one by one.
Which one grabs hold of you most? Why? Journal your thoughts and meditations.

3. As Bible teacher Michael McKay says,
"When we think about our own mortality, we often like to push that off as much as possible...I think it's healthy for us to think about it before it happens, because it causes us to ask the big questions in life." [61]

Prayerfully consider what you would like your last words to be.
Talk to the Lord about it.
Jot down your thoughts and feelings in your journal.

53. DIY: Living in Christ as Life

…your real life is hidden with Christ in God.
And when Christ, who is your life, is revealed to the whole world,
you will share in all his glory.
Colossians 3:3b-4 NLT

We are such a "Do It Yourself" society. DIY projects with instructions abound on the Internet. Some are very useful, like baking your own bread and organizing a closet. Some can be quite time consuming, like scrapbooking and renovating a bedroom. And others can be downright frustrating, like losing weight or styling your own hair. So it seems we are always looking for the key, the formula, the hint that will make us go, "Aha!"

This is also true for our spiritual life. We are always thinking the latest Christian "best seller," the current popular discipleship program, the "hottest" Christian speaker or author will have the answer. They will have the key to all our struggles and frustrations in living the Christian life.

Well, sisters and brothers, I have good news. I have the key to the Christian life. And you do too. Because Christianity is a Person, not a procedure; the Lord, not a list. Not church attendance, not Christ-like qualities, not good works, not the Christian "to-do list" (which may vary depending on the group and "camp" you are in).

Not evangelism, not mission trips, not a quality "quiet time," not Scripture memorization or Bible study. Not spiritual disciplines, not prayer, not fasting, not obedience, not miracle-working faith. Not ______________________ (you fill in the blank with your favorite supposed "godliness-producing external" activity).

In other words, not our desperate trying by our own efforts to be and do and get God to love us more. No.

> The LORD JESUS CHRIST, the Son of God. The Lord Jesus...HE is the Christian life.

In fact, He is the key to everything. And it's not just what He's done for us, as total and complete as that is. No, it's His very Person. He is our very Life.

> *Christ died for us,*
> *so that He could give His life to us,*
> *so that He could live His life in us and through us...*
> *as us, not as some illustrious Christian we admire, not as*
> *some super-person.*

He lives in us to live the "Christian life" through us. That's because He's the only one able to live it. He is God's *Amen* and total sum of all things. And the amazing thing is, He lives in me. And He lives in you too, O child of God, through faith in this glorious Son of God.

> ...God has chosen to make known...the glorious riches of this mystery, which is Christ in you, the hope of glory.
> Colossians 1:27 NIV

The Treasure who indwells us by faith in His Stellar Self is none other than our Lord and Savior Jesus Christ, the Son of God.

> ...the glory of God…is seen in the face of Jesus Christ. We now have this light shining in our hearts, but we ourselves are

like fragile clay jars containing this great treasure. This makes
it clear that our great power is from God, not from ourselves.
2 Corinthians 4:6-7 NLT

Our Lord Jesus is the Father's All in All. And He will live through
us, as us, as we let Him -- as we in faith depend on Him.

May we begin to see those spiritual activities, that we think are the
Christian life, fall into perspective (and some may even fall away) in
light of all that He is—everything and anything we will ever need.

For in Christ lives all the fullness of God in a human body. So
you also are complete [full] through your union with Christ,
who is the head over every ruler and authority.
Colossians 2:9-10 NLT

May this become our equation for life:
JESUS + nothing = Everything

True Life's Key
How is it that I'll ever be free
Of my self-conscious search
For who I should be?

How will I ever find true liberty
With my fear of the future
And what it might be?

But I know the One
Who holds true life's key
For the Risen Christ has paid my fee,

For my past, present & future reality.
It's His life He's living
Through me as me!
       Penny Mandeville

<u>Prayer</u>
Lord, You know how I've spent so much of my life as a believer searching for what I already have – the Key to not only the Christian Life but to all of life. Thank You for your forgiveness and Your indwelling Presence that was there all along. Teach me to live in total dependence on You Who lives in me and through me as I let You. In Your name. Amen.

<u>Reflections</u>
1. List the "formulas, steps, programs" you have gone through during your time as a believer. What Bible studies have you done, in person or online? Thank the Lord for what you learned through each of those.

2. Were there any that you did out of an attitude of trying to earn something with God or because "that's what good Christians do" — performance based?
Thank Him for His already-forgiveness for any "God substitutes." Embrace afresh the simplicity that is Christ.

3. Read the Gospel of John this week and make note of the descriptions of your Jesus that grab hold of your mind and heart. Bask in Him Who is your Everything, your very Life.

4. I love this verse. It has become a reminder for me:

But I fear, lest somehow, as the serpent deceived Eve by his craftiness, so your minds may be corrupted from <u>the simplicity that is in Christ</u>.
2 Corinthians 11:3 NKJV (emphasis added)

GLORY IN SPECIAL DAYS

...the awareness of Christ's present risenness
persuades us that we are buoyed up
and carried on by a life greater than our own...
He is our life, the most real fact about us.[62]
Brennan Manning
The Rabbi's Heartbeat

54. Easter Bonnets: Walking in Newness of Life

I am the Resurrection and the Life;
he who believes in Me shall live even if he dies,
and everyone who lives and believes in Me shall never die.
John 11:25-26 NASB

I have two younger sisters, Linda and Nancy. At Easter every year, our mom would dress us up in our ruffly new Easter dresses, shoes, purses, and of course, bonnets.

Oh those beautiful bonnets! Since I am the oldest of the three, my Easter bonnets were always brand new. My younger sisters, on the other hand, often had my hand-me-downs, decorated to make them "new to them."

My youngest sister Nancy loves to tell the story of our bonnets this way (with some "poetic license," of course).

> "Janet's bonnet was always new, with a brim full of flowers all around. Linda's bonnet was Janet's 'last year's bonnet,' but minus the flowers (which probably had fallen apart over the course of the year).

> So by the time it got to me, the bonnet was just the crown, with maybe a bit of ribbon around it to 'dress it up.' But believe it or not, I always loved that bonnet."

But Easter isn't about bonnets and ruffly dresses, is it? It's not about bunnies, chicks, colored eggs, Easter lilies or other spring flowers. They are all simply pictures, metaphors, if you will, of the real deal. And the real deal is life, new life.

Easter is about our Lord's new, up from the grave, Resurrection Life. He conquered sin and death on the cross and then was raised, so that we could walk in newness of His Life.

> Jesus Himself said, "I am the way, and the truth, and the life." John 14:6 ESV

Christ's life is *God's Life*—spiritual life, not physical. His Life is uncreated, eternal, indestructible, unchanging. How does God's own eternal Life happen for you and me? It can only happen one way – through union with Him who is Life Himself through the new birth.

> Jesus said, "Truly, truly, I say to you, unless one is born again, he cannot see the kingdom of God." John 3:3 ESV

And this Life is not just enough to get us into heaven.
No. Christ's Life is abundant, over the top, more than sufficient for life on earth—right here, right now.

> Jesus said, "I came that they may have life, and that they may have it abundantly." John 10:10 ESV

So hear the good news of the Gospel:

> *Jesus Christ, the Son of God, died <u>for</u> you.*
> *So that He could give His life <u>to</u> you,*
> *In order to live His life <u>through</u> you, as you.*

Not just on Easter, but every day of the year, dear child of God, meditate on this glorious thought—the Resurrected Christ is alive in your world right now. The Living Christ lives in you today. And this same Lord Jesus Christ lives His resurrection life through you as you walk in "present risen-ness" every day.

Easter Morning

It's Easter Morning and I want to shout!
What is it I want to shout about?

Not about tulips and chocolate bunnies,
Or colored eggs full of gummy bear yummies.

But because Your tomb was empty that morning
And that put an end to Your followers' mourning.

Though You suffered and died upon that cross
You rose in Victory for all who were lost.

Even though we certainly didn't deserve it
For we did absolutely nothing to earn it.

For it is a fact that we were all sinners
But You, by Your sacrifice, made us all winners.

For we're the recipients of Your love and grace
Not by our intelligence, our actions, or our race.

Let us not forget in all today's busy-ness
To thank You and celebrate Your present risen-ness.
      Penny Mandeville

Prayer

Lord Jesus, live through me, love through me, serve through me today. Unfold the fullness of Your Resurrection Life in and through me today. For Your glory and purpose in this generation. Amen.

.

<u>Reflections</u>

1. In a very real sense, every day is Easter, Resurrection Day, for those of us who are alive with His Life. Reflect on the various traditions, symbols of new life that abound in your family or community celebration of Easter. Journal each one and what aspect of new life is pictured there.

2. Get a set of "Resurrection Eggs."
Share the story of the death and resurrection of Christ with children or your friends. What fresh revelations came out of your discussion?

3. Get an empty basket and each day (morning &/or evening), place your pressing concerns into the basket – even write them out specifically and date them. Leave them with the Risen Christ. He can carry them. You and I can't. Later, take a peek at those daily concerns and journal what the Lord did when they were given over to Him. (Thank you, Beth Loyd Filson, for this marvelous idea.)

55. Thanksgiving: Overflowing with Gratitude

Therefore as you have received Christ Jesus the Lord,
so walk in Him,
having been firmly rooted and now being built up in Him
and established in your faith, just as you were instructed,
and overflowing with gratitude.
Colossians 2:6-7 NASB

Years ago, I taught writing to adult GED students. Every Wednesday, we would do an exercise together as a class to practice writing a five-paragraph essay. As the end of November approached, I chose the topic of *Thanksgiving.* I thought that in this age of "entitlement" it might be a double "win" for the students to count their blessings and practice their writing.

So to prepare for my lesson, I sent out an email to gather quotes about being thankful from friends and colleagues. I received some great ones. Some were fun:

> *What we're really talking about is a wonderful day set aside on the fourth Thursday of November when no one diets. I mean, why else would they call it Thanksgiving?"*
> Erma Bombeck

> *May your stuffing be tasty.*
> *May your turkey be plump.*
> *May your potatoes and gravy*
> *Have nary a lump.*
> *May your yams be delicious,*
> *And may your pies take the prize,*
> *And may your Thanksgiving dinner,*

Stay off your thighs!
Anonymous

Others were really profound:
Gratitude is the least of the virtues, but ingratitude is the worst of the vices.
Thomas Fuller

The pilgrims made seven times more graves than huts…nevertheless, they set aside a day of thanksgiving.
H.W.Westermayer

A thankful heart is not only the greatest virtue, but the parent of all the others.
Cicero

My favorite:
It's not the happy person who is thankful but the thankful person who is happy.
Anonymous

As always, God's Word takes the prize for the most sublime quote on being thankful.

Therefore as you have received Christ Jesus the Lord, so walk in Him, having been firmly instructed, and <u>overflowing with gratitude</u>.
Colossians 2:6-7 NASB (emphasis added)

How I love that final phrase, *overflowing with gratitude*. How picturesque.

What does it mean to overflow? It makes me think of a story my husband John tells about growing up in Arizona near a reservoir, Roosevelt Dam. When it rained too much or the snows in the mountains began to melt, the water flowed over the edge of the dam. John remembers what an event it was for him as a child when the dam spilled over. It was a wonder to behold. And that's what this word in the original language means, "to be in excess, to have more than enough, to super-abound -- to overflow."

And what is *gratitude*? It's an "emotion of the heart, excited by a favor or benefit received; a sentiment of kindness or good will towards a benefactor; thanksgiving." (Webster, 1828).

After all, "what do you have that you did not receive?"
(See 1 Corinthians 4:7).

The original word in Greek is "eucharistia." In Christian liturgical traditions,

> "Eucharist" is used in modern language for Holy Communion, embodying the highest act of thanksgiving for the greatest gift from God, the sacrifice of Jesus. It is the grateful acknowledgement of past mercies.[63]

In fact, Jesus Himself gave thanks to the Father as He broke the bread and blessed the cup at the Last Supper with His disciples. He acknowledged His Father as the Giver of "every good gift and every perfect gift" (James 1:17). And this ordinance or in some traditions, "sacrament," of the church is often referred to as the "Holy Eucharist."

So let us also, dear brothers and sisters, be a people *overflowing with gratitude,* always, every day of our lives. After all, what do we have, that we have not received from the Gift-giver Himself?

Thankful

How many ways can we thank You, Dear One
For all that we have and for all You have done?

You've given us life
And sustained us each day.

Our hearts and our minds
Bow to You as we pray.

You are our shelter
Through every storm.

You hold us close
In Your arms, safe and warm.

With hearts full of worship
We offer You praise.

With love and Thanksgiving
All of our days!
      Penny Mandeville

Prayer

Lord God, Giver of every gift, I confess my blindness to Your goodnesses, big and small. Open my eyes and move my heart to overflowing gratitude in everything You send my way. Amen.

<u>Reflections</u>

1. What 5 things can you thank God for right now? In your journal, list them. Then chose one of the 5 and list 5 more related to that one. Keep going if you'd like … and never stop listing.

2. Do this Bible study exercise: Read through the book of Colossians and find at least one verse in each chapter about giving thanks. Be sure to read the context to get the complete message.

3. Have a time of family or personal communion, thanking the Father for the gift of His precious Son.

56. The Christmas Cake: Tasting the Sweetness of Emmanuel

Taste and see that the LORD is good.
How happy is the man who takes refuge in Him.
Psalm 34:8 CSB

I had good intentions. The recipe looked easy enough, yet festive: chocolate orange cake. I figured that this year the grandsons were old enough to enjoy a birthday for Jesus. And who doesn't like chocolate? Even though I had been tempted by the beautiful little chocolate cake at Trader Joe's, I decided to take the plunge myself. I pulled out the springform pan and went at it.

I wasn't prepared for the result. Even though my toothpick came out clean, something happened to part of the middle as it cooled on the rack. If the whole middle had sunk a little, it wouldn't have been that bad. But there it was, a desperately misshapen birthday cake for Jesus. My efforts at patching it up just ended in making it worse: glaze sliding off one side, crumbs in the glaze . . . nothing I tried helped. Discouraged, pressured, and ready to pitch the thing and go spend $7.99 for that cute little TJ cake…

I remembered Jesus.

I realized that he *never* had a perfect birthday cake (if they even did that in those days). Even his actual birth-day was far from perfect…no hospital, no doctor, no nursery with a clean crib and changing table, no doting relatives, no baby showers, no "home sweet home," not even a room in a hotel; but rather a barn filled with animals, far from loved ones, with two teenaged parents, and unclean outcasts with their sheep for visitors. Of course, God couldn't resist throwing in a few angels and a star. But they were only visible to the few believing hearts.

Something began to change in my attitude toward my cake. Now it was a picture, a metaphor, for my lovely Lord who wasn't one of the beautiful people:

> He had no form or majesty that we should look at him, and no beauty that we should desire him.
> Isaiah 53:2 ESV

My cake began to speak to me of this glorious One who came to earth and put up with a broken, imperfect life for my sake:

> And the Word became flesh and dwelt [pitched his tent] among us, and we saw his glory, glory as of the only begotten from the Father, full of grace and truth.
> John 1:14 NASB (emphasis added)

> Have this attitude in yourselves which was also in Christ Jesus, who although He existed in the form of God…emptied Himself, taking the form of a bond-servant…and humbled Himself by becoming obedient to the point of death, even death on a cross.
> Philippians 2:5–8 NASB

So I swallowed my pride and put a little crystal nativity on top. When it was time for dessert, I read the verse from Isaiah, and we sang "Happy Birthday" to Jesus. The funny thing is that my little misshapen cake was actually delicious…kinda like Jesus, huh?

<u>My Worth Comes from You</u>
I may not be pretty
I may not be smart
I may not be talented
In sports or in art.

Never wrote a book
Or published a song
But my worth comes from knowing
To whom I belong.

I have learned this truth
Through many life lessons
That nothing compares
With being in His presence.
            Penny Mandeville

<u>Prayer</u>
LORD, I confess I am focused more often on achieving perfection than on worshiping You, my humble Savior. Thank You for taking on my brokenness, so I could take on Your holiness. Transform me more and more into Your likeness as I rest in You. Amen.

<u>Reflections</u>
1. When holiday preparations of any kind are in process, do you become a "crazy person" from stress-filled perfectionism? Can you relinquish these preparations to the Lord, asking for His perspective and empowering? Journal your thoughts and prayer to Him.

2. What is your favorite Christmas song, celebrating Immanuel, God With Us? Research the backstory for the song. Find the lyrics and /or a video online and sing it to your Lord with all your heart.

57. Epiphany: Shining Light or Drama Queen?

> … the people who sat in darkness have seen a great light.
> And for those who lived in the land where death casts its shadow,
> a light has shined.
> Matthew 4:15-16 NLT

On January 6th, many Christians celebrate the feast of the *Epiphany*. It's the day on the church calendar that "commemorates the visit of the Magi to the Christ Child and the revelation of God the Son as a human being."

The Wise Men or Magi were Gentiles who came from afar following a star…

> Now after Jesus was born in Bethlehem of Judea in the days of Herod the king, magi from the east arrived in Jerusalem, saying, "Where is He who has been born King of the Jews? For we saw His star in the east and have come to worship Him...
> …they went their way; and the star, which they had seen in the east, went on before them until it came and stood over the place where the Child was.
> When they saw the star, they rejoiced exceedingly with great joy.
> Matthew 2:1-2,11-12 ESV

Those Wise Men, those star-gazers (a.k.a. astrologers) sure did get a humdinger of a star. It was a special star leading the way to a King, but not just any king. He is the King of kings and Lord of lords. So this star pointed to the Presence of deity, an "epiphany," a revelation. Jesus Himself is the manifestation of deity in human form.

He said of Himself,

> I am the light of the world. Whoever follows me will not walk in darkness, but will have the light of life.
> John 8:12 ESV

But guess what? He also said of us believers,

> You are the light of the world. A town built on a hill cannot be hidden. Neither do people light a lamp and put it under a bowl. Instead, they put it on its stand, and it gives light to everyone in the house. In the same way, let your light shine before others, that they may see your good deeds and glorify your Father in heaven.   Mathew 5:14-16 NIV

That means we are like the star that led the Magi to Christ…or we *can be*. We can, in our very person, be the light that points another to the King. You and I have the King of kings living within us. But as always it is our choice whether we allow the King to live through us and manifest His presence to seeking hearts who are walking in darkness all around us.

Author Tim Chester, in his lovely Advent devotional on Philippians, *The One True Gift*,[64] caught my attention when he pointed out from Scripture one way God says we can shine like stars:

> Do everything without grumbling or arguing, so that you may become blameless and pure,

"children of God without fault in a warped and crooked
generation."
Then you will shine among them like stars in the sky
as you hold firmly to the word of life.
Philippians 2:15-16 NIV

Ouch. Not grumbling, not arguing…not complaining, not being a
"drama queen," but yielding to the indwelling Christ to live His light
of life in and through me in the situation at hand. Then I will shine
like a star who points to the King of my life. He is the King of the
world.

How about you, my sister? My brother?

> For God, who said, "Let light shine out of darkness," made
> his light shine in our hearts to give us the light of the
> knowledge of God's glory displayed in the face of Christ.
> But we have this treasure in jars of clay
> to show that this all-surpassing power is from God and not
> from us.
> We are hard pressed on every side, but not crushed;
> perplexed, but not in despair;
> persecuted, but not abandoned;
> struck down, but not destroyed.
> We always carry around in our body the death of Jesus,
> so that the life of Jesus may also be revealed in our body.
> For we who are alive are always being given over to death
> for Jesus' sake,
> so that his life may also be revealed in our mortal body.
> So then, death is at work in us, but life is at work in you.
> 2 Corinthians 4:6-12 NIV

May we be an *epiphany* for others in our daily lives as we let the Living Christ manifest Himself through us wherever we are.

<u>What Do I Portray?</u>
I wonder as I walk through life
Just what the world might see.

Do I portray a grumpy grump?
Or a prisoner set free?

Am I full of darkness
Discouraged and afraid?

Or do they see a soul set free
By the price that You have paid?

Oh, let me be a testament
Of your unending grace!

May they see Your love in me
When they look into my face!
       Penny Mandeville

<u>Prayer</u>
O dear Lord, the Light of the world, may it be so in my life today. May You and Your glorious presence be manifest as revelation to those around me. And let them know it's You. In your shining Name. Amen.

<u>Reflections</u>
Ask the Holy Spirit to pull you up short when you begin to complain…or when you enter into the complaining and drama of

others around you. Respond to Him as He opens your mind and heart to His perspective. Remember, complaining is contagious but so also is gratitude.

GLORY IN OUR STORY

No matter how ordinary a person may be,
put God in that person,
and the ordinary becomes extraordinary.[65]
Major W. Ian Thomas,
The Indwelling Life of Christ

58. Jan's Journey: Seeing His Smile

See what great love the Father has lavished on us,
that we should be called children of God!
And that is what we are.
1 John 3:1 NLT

Much of my life I lived under the "frown of God," or so I thought. I wasn't a bad kid; in fact, I was quite religious and moral. But I wasn't perfect for sure. For one thing, I wasn't a very loving or kind big sister. I was self-centered and heartless. And I knew God required perfection, so I was always working my way down a spiritual "to do list" of some kind.

My heart was tender toward God, but my concept of Him was off. I thought He was waiting for my perfect performance. Even though I had come to understand and embrace the unconditional grace of God for salvation, I continued to make lists of my own to make me "spiritual." I wanted to be more pleasing to God so that He would love me more, use me more, and not frown so much. I had a prayer list for each day, week, and month; fasting days; a scripture memorization schedule; Bible study plan, etc. etc.

I was sincere. But I was always wondering if I "qualified" to get God's help to be and do what He wanted. I was a Christian, and I wasn't working for my salvation. I knew that I was secure because of my Lord and Savior Jesus Christ. Rather, this was my askew, "messed up" way of living. This was the "Christian life," I thought.

Then after years of this sin-focused, legalistic, unproductive way of living; after years of struggle with a mixture of grace and "Christian law;" after failing health because of strange sensitivities and years of being thought of as a hypochondriac; I finally gave up. I assumed

God was judging me, but I basically said to the Lord, "I can't do this anymore."

That's when I heard the Voice and saw *the Smile that destroyed my religion*. My Father through His indwelling Spirit, said to my heart:

"I love you even if you never do another thing right."

When I chose to believe and embrace this message as God's truth for my life, everything changed. In an instant my soul was set free by the unconditional love of God -- His "*Never Stopping, Never Giving Up, Unbreaking, Always and Forever Love.*"[66]

I felt like I was born again, again. I began seeing God's love and grace all over the scriptures. I hadn't really "seen" His love there before. His love remained hidden, because I was focused on the "doing" passages and not the "done" passages—not on the truth verses, like these:

See what great love the Father has lavished on us, that we should be called children of God! And that is what we are! The reason the world does not know us is that it did not know him. Dear friends, now we are children of God, and what we will be has not yet been made known. But we know that when Christ appears, we shall be like him, for we shall see him as he is.   1 John 3:1-2 NLT

The Father Himself loves you.   John 16:27 NASB

I am convinced that neither death, nor life, nor angels, nor principalities, nor things present, nor things to come, nor powers, nor height, nor depth, nor any other created thing, shall be able to separate us from the love of God, which is in Christ Jesus our Lord.   Romans 8:38–39 NASB

And so besides seeing Love all over the pages of God's Word, I began to see His Smile–it was there all the time. Now I live under that Smile. I live in Grace, no longer law or a mix of law and grace...just grace.

What about you, my friend? Are you living under what you think is God's frown or even His fickleness ("He loves me/He loves me not"). Those are lies from the pit. Embrace God and His unconditional love: His "*Never Stopping, Never Giving Up, Unbreaking, Always and Forever Love.*"[55]

Live under His Smile and in pure grace because that is your reality, O child of God. Then He can transform you by His indwelling Holy Spirit of Life.

God's Smile
To see a loved one's smiling face
Is like receiving a Valentine trimmed with lace
Or visiting a friendly, homey place,
Or getting a lovely warm embrace.

Can you imagine God's smiling face?
Looking at you He sees not a trace
Of your failures, short comings or disgrace
Because He sees you through His love and Grace.
         Penny Mandeville

Prayer
O my Father God, thank You for speaking Your smiling words that set my soul free from my faulty religion – my checklists, my trying

to earn what I already have. I now know that your unconditional, tender love for me, your beloved daughter, is fixed. Nothing has been the same since. I see Your smile always and never your frown. Your love is no longer hidden from my sight. And it's all Your Son's doing. So for me it's done. Amen.

Reflections

1. Do you see God smiling at you or frowning or changing back and forth? If His expression is frowning or changing, what do you think is causing that?

2. Are you on the verge of giving up? Take the risk and fling it all on Him. Then embrace the Truth and hear the Voice and see the Smile that will set you free.

3. As you meditate on the above Scriptures, ask the Holy Spirit to make His unconditional love and grace real to you in the depths of your soul. Amen.

59. Penny's Pictures: Surrendering to His Sovereignty

So humble yourselves under the mighty power of God,
and at the right time he will lift you up in honor.
Give all your worries and cares to God, for he cares about you.
1 Peter 5:6-7 NLT

I am more than excited for you to hear from Penny, our resident poet, as she tells her personal story of God's revelation at a very critical time.

Penny and I have been friends for many years. We have studied the Word of God together during most of that time. I'll never forget Penny's comment one Bible study morning—"God's Word is so delicious." Penny is one of the most humble and spiritually sensitive people I know. She knows how to hear God, which is obvious in her poetry.

When I asked Penny what she would want readers to know about her, she replied, "I don't have a lot of accomplishments. Maybe about being married for 51 years, 3 children, 7 grandchildren. I love walking through nature, reading, coloring. I love the Lord."

Whew, we women know there are accomplishments galore in that statement.

Now, here is my sweet friend and our resident poet Penny Mandeville in her own words:

> The Lord gave me a word for the year. At first I thought it was for someone else. But then I heard the Lord say, "No. This word is for you, Penny!" The word was "Surrender".

Surrender. Not a very uplifting word.

Just before Christmas 2020, I was diagnosed with breast cancer. I wasn't devastated but I was truly surprised. So, in the new year I wasn't sure how the year would unfold. I asked the Lord,

"How will I figure it all out?"

The answer I heard? "Surrender."

But what does surrender look like? These are the three images that came to mind:

> The first was a person with hands raised in the air. Like in a cowboy movie. 'Stick 'em up!' Surrender.

> The second was on a battle field, a soldier flying a white flag. Surrender.

> The third was a person laying down their weapon. Surrender."

Those three images were very defeatist. Depressing. Especially after receiving the diagnosis of cancer.

Then I felt the Lord urge me to take a closer look.

> As I zeroed in I saw that I was the one with hands raised. But I wasn't surrendering to the enemy. I was raising my hands in worship to God. I was surrendering in worship to the Father. My Father in

Heaven. He has the big picture. He saw this cancer coming and knows what to do with it. I can trust Him never to leave me or forsake me. I lift my hands in worship to Him.

In the second image I held a flag but not a flag of surrender to the enemy. The flag was to signify the presence of my king. Our British friend Julie once told us that when the King was in residence, they flew his flag over the castle. I realized the flag meant the Holy Spirit was present in me. That flag acknowledges the presence of the Holy Spirit. My counselor, my comforter. When I acknowledge His presence in me, I have that peace that goes beyond understanding.

In the third image I lay down my weapons, not in defeat but in understanding that I don't have the weapons to fight this battle. This battle belongs to Jesus. He is my healer. He is the warrior. I lay down my human weapons and trust Jesus to lead me down the right path of healing through this battle.

My part in this was to worship the Father, to acknowledge the Holy Spirit and to trust Jesus. To surrender.

There were times through this process that weren't fun. Times it was uncomfortable. Times I had to do things I didn't want to do. But it helped knowing I wasn't the one in charge. I had already made the decision to surrender, to trust Jesus. I knew if He truly didn't want me to do what the doctors were suggesting He would give me that feeling of "no, no, no!" But all I heard was, "Trust Me. I'm right here with you!"

I am now finished with my treatment. I've had chemotherapy, surgery and radiation. Along the way I've met many people who have had a much more difficult time in treatment than I have. I don't mean to make light of having cancer. And I know that if my outcome had been different that God would still be good! I have had many friends and loved ones praying for me. I am so thankful for their support. I am truly grateful for this experience. It has shown me another layer of trusting God and knowing Jesus is with me. There is such freedom in surrendering to Him.

My Surrender

When I am alone
You are my befriender.
In the heat of battle
You are my defender.
To my broken heart
You are the mender.
I need never be
a pretender,
Because all to You
I surrender.

       Penny Mandeville

Prayer

Dear Heavenly Father, I thank You for loving me and always going before me. You know what's ahead for me. I worship you with all my heart.

Holy Spirit, thank You for always being with me. Help me to remember to acknowledge Your presence. I praise You.

Precious Jesus, thank You for always being my protector and

leading me down the right path. I know I can trust You. I love You!
I surrender all to You. Amen.

<u>Reflections</u>
1. Can you think of a time when you had to blindly trust Jesus and
surrender to Him the process and the outcome?

2. Are you now going through a situation you must surrender to
Him? It can be very hard to do, but I encourage you to do so. There
is so much freedom in surrendering to Him. You can trust Him
because He cares for you.

60. Your Story: Remembering His Revelation

Remember the wonders he has performed,
his miracles, and the rulings he has given.
Psalm 105:5 NLT

Each of us is on a unique journey and has a story to tell. Our journey-stories are filled with highs and lows, adventures and crises, and everything in between.

Author Anne Lamott says that some have chosen "to see the world sacramentally, to see everything as an outward and visible sign of inward, invisible grace."[67]

So God reveals Himself in and through even the mundane of our lives. But maybe you have had a hard time seeing that, until now. We pray God has used your time with us in this little volume to show how He has been with you and in you and in your story all along also.

Perhaps now is the time to begin writing your faith journey. When I started journaling mine, I was motivated by thinking,

> "Oh how I wish my godly grandmother and my godly mother had kept a journal or had written of their journey with God through the trials of life."

But alas, they had not. And it was most likely not possible for them. But it was possible for me, so I began.

We pray you will take the risk and begin. Tell your story in whatever genre (poetry or prose), whatever style you desire. Even in bits and pieces and sporadically will be beneficial. Write in the "nooks and crannies of time" in your life. Don't get sucked into a perfectionistic trap.

May God bless you in your writing. May you see "His Smile" (Jan), and may you receive His "pictures" (Penny) as you go along. Your children and grandchildren will thank you. And you may find that in the writing, you meet God afresh in the midst of your stuff—undisguised.

His Plan
Each day is a picture
Of God as the Victor
Of all the challenges we face.

We may not see His hand
As He works out His plan
But He's helping us run our race.

He's always been there
Whether or not we're aware
No matter the time or place

Each life tells the tale
Of God's strength when we're frail
And His Blessings of Love and His Grace!
      Penny Mandeville

Prayer
Write out your own prayer to God. Ask Him about this suggestion to record your journey. Listen for His answer and respond.

Reflections
Here are a few questions to get you started:

1. What are some of your earliest memories?

2. Was there a significant person, place, truth that impacted you
    in your early years?

3. What were your turning points in life? Jot them down. You
    can go back and process with the Lord later. My story told of
    a significant spiritual turning point in my life. There have
    been others. So whether hugely significant or not, record
    them. You never know what God may reveal to you.

4. What were some of the lovely things in your life? Can you
    see God in those things?
    Thank Him.

5. What were some of the hard things that happened in your
    life?
    Process them with the Lord. Thank Him even for those.
    Penny's story told of a physical crisis in her life and what
    God gave her to see her through triumphantly.
    Ask the Lord to show you where He was in the midst of your
    trial.
    Watch how God takes your struggles and trials, as time goes
    on, and reveals truths about Himself and about your life that
    you can build upon.

6. Go back through your journal from this journey with us. Do
    you see a pattern? Have you seen God working in your life
    in specific ways? Incorporate those into your stories.

So just start writing or journaling your thoughts — no need to write
it up formally. I started out with events and memories and

significant people, etc. And little by little, God revealed Himself and some of what He was doing at that time.

Remember, *God and His Glory* are often hidden, even disguised, in your ordinary life.

He is in your narrative.
Ask Him to open your eyes to see Him there.

ENDNOTES

[1]Richard Foster. "The Incarnational Tradition: Discovering the Sacramental Life," *Streams of Living Water.* (San Francisco: HarperCollins, 1998), 237.

[2]Henri Nouwen. *The Living Reminder*: *Service and Prayer in Memory of Jesus Christ.*
(San Francisco: HarperCollins, 1977).

[3]Brennan Manning. *Abba's Child.* (Colorado Springs: NavPress, 2015).

[4]Anne Lamott. *Bird by Bird.* (New York: Anchor Books, 1994), 100-101.

[5]Henri Nouwen. *Life of the Beloved: Spiritual Living in a Secular World* (New York: Crossroad Publishing, 1992), 28.

[6]Mark Maulding. *God's Best-Kept Secret: Christianity Is Easier Than You Think.* (Grand Rapids: Baker Books, 2017), 73-74.

[7]*"Fiddler on the Roof.* Sunrise, Sunset." Accessed July 22, 2023. *https://www.streetdirectory.com/lyricadvisor/song/wplfoe/sunrise_sunset/.*

[8]Author Unknown. "Unfolding the Rose," Sarah Y. Accessed July 23, 2023. https://medium.com/@SarahY./unfolding-the-rose-198a14b5c91e.

[9]Brennan Manning. *Abba's Child.*

[10]"Be Thou My Vision." Accessed July 23, 2023. https://hymnary.org/text/be_thou_my_vision_o_lord_of_my_heart.

[11]"Morning Has Broken." Accessed July 23, 2023. https://hymnary.org/text/morning_has_broken.

[12]Sally Lloyd-Jones, JAGO (illustrator). *The Jesus Storybook Bible: Every Story Whispers His Name.* (Grand Rapids: Zonderkids, c2007).

[13]Dolly Parton. "God's Coloring Book." Accessed July 18, 2023. https://www.lyrics.com/lyric/9112816/Dolly+Parton/God%27s+Coloring+Book.

[14]"Laughter Really is the Best Medicine." Source unknown.

[15]John Trent & Gary Smalley. *The Blessing.* (New York: POCKET BOOKS, 1982).

[16]Major W. Ian Thomas. *The Indwelling Life of Christ.* (Colorado Springs: Multnomah Books, 2006).

[17]Brennan Manning, *Abba's Child*

[18]Jill Briscoe. *The DEEP PLACE Where Nobody Goes.* (Oxford, UK: Monarch Books, c2005).

[19]Christine Wyrtzen. *Daughters of Promise.* Accessed July 23, 2023. https://daughtersofpromise.org.

[20]Major W. Ian Thomas. *The Indwelling Life of Christ*, 99.

[21]Andrew Murray. *The True Vine.* (USA: The Whitaker House, 1982).

[22]James K.A. Smith. *You Are What You Love.* (Grand Rapids: Brazos Press, 2016).

[23]The Carpenters. "I Won't Last a Day Without You." AZ Lyrics. https://www.azlyrics.com/lyrics/carpenters/iwontlastadaywithoutyou.html.

[24]Kenny Rogers. "Through the Years." AZ Lyrics. Accessed July 24, 2023. https://www.azlyrics.com/lyrics/kennyrogers/throughtheyears.html.

[25]Travis Cottrell. "Annie's Song." LYRICS. Accessed July 24, 2023. https://www.lyrics.com/lyric/9764604/Travis+Cottrell.

[26]Whiteheart. "We Are His Hands." LYRICS. Accessed July 24, 2023. https://www.lyrics.com/lyric/7251671/We+Are+His+Hands.

[27]Rankin Wilbourne, *Union with Christ.* (Colorado Springs: David C. Cook, 2016), 101.

[28]C.S. Lewis, *Mere Christianity.* (New York: Macmillan Company, 1952), V.4.

[29]Brennan Manning, *Abba's Child.*

[30]James G. Friesen, E. James Wilder, Anne M. Bierling, Rick Koepcke, Maribeth Poole.

Living from the Hear Jesus Gave You. (Pasadena: Shepherd's House, 2004).

[31]Corrie ten Boom. *Tramp for the Lord.* (New York: Berkley Books, 1974).

[32]Wikipedia. "Salt in the Bible." Accessed July 22, 2023. https://en.wikipedia.org/wiki/Salt_in_the_Bible.

[33]Richard Rohr. *Everything Belongs.* (New York: The Crossroad Publishing Company, 1971).

[34]Pete Briscoe. *Life in Christ Media*, Inc., New Berlin, Wisconsin. info@petebriscoe.org.

[35]Brennan Manning, *Abba's Child.*

[36]William Blake. Accessed July 24, 2023. https://www.brainyquote.com/authors/william-blake-quotes.

[37]Laura Detico, Wayne McLoughlin. *God Says I Am: What God Tells About Himself in the Bible—from A to Z.* (Cincinnati: Standard Publishing, c2002).

[38]A.W. Tozer. *Pursuit of God.* (Harrisburg, PA: Christian Publications, Inc, 1948).

[39]The Beatles. "Yesterday." Genius. Accessed July 18, 2023. https://genius.com/The-beatles-yesterday-lyrics.

[40]*Annie.* "Tomorrow." ST LYRICS. Accessed July 18, 2023. https://www.stlyrics.com/lyrics/annie/tomorrow.htm.

[41]Carol McCloud. *Have You Filled a Bucket Today?* Accessed July 24, 2023. www.bucketfillers.com.

[42]A.A. Milne quotes. Winnie the Pooh. "Today." Facebook 2021.

[43]Mike Q. Daniel. https://mikeqdaniel.com.

[44]Mark & Patti Virkler. *Counseled by God.* (LamadPublishing@cluonline.com 2002).

[45]Marshall, Catherine. "The Prayer of Relinquishment." *Guideposts.* https://guideposts.org/prayer/prayers-for-stronger-faith/the-prayer-of-relinquishment/.

[46]Gravitt, Justin. "Pandemic Disciple-Making." https://www.justingravitt.com/blog/pandemic-darkness.

[47]John Piper. "The Image of God: An Approach from Biblical and Systematic Theology" (*Studia Biblica et Tehologica*, March 1971, www.desiringgod.org/ResourceLibrary/Articles/ByDate/1971/22271

[48]http://www.monologuedb.com/monologues-for-kids-/the-wizard-of-oz-the-cowardly-lion/.

[49]Jerry Seinfeld. *Jerry Seinfeld Quotes & Sayings.* https://www.inspiringquotes.us/author/9593-jerry-seinfeld/page:2.

[50]GLAD. "Where Can I Go." Genius. Accessed July 18, 2023. https://genius.com/Glad-where-can-i-go-lyrics.

[51]Sandra Bullock. "The Best Sandra Bullock Quotes." *The Power of Positivity.* https://fb.watch/luT0eTfs7t/.

[52]Roy Lesson. "Above All," *Dayspring Journal* (www.dayspring.com).

[53]Getty, Keith & Kristen. "He Will Hold Me Fast." Genius. Accessed July 18,2023. https://genius.com/Keith-and-kristyn-getty-he-will-hold-me-fast-live-sing-2019-edition-lyrics.

[54]Francis, S. Trevor. "O the Deep, Deep Love of Jesus." Hymnary.org. Accessed July 18, 2023. https://hymnary.org/text/o_the_deep_deep_love_of_jesus.

[55]Charles Spurgeon. Facebook.

[56]Stuart Briscoe. *Telling the Truth* newsletter, May 1999.

[57]Joyce Kilmer. "The House with Nobody in It." Famous Poets and Poems. Accessed July 18, 2023. http://famouspoetsandpoems.com/poets/joyce_kilmer/poems/17339.

[58]Dr. Wayne Barber. *The Rest of Grace* (Eugene, OR: Harvest House Publishers, 1998), 14.

[59]Pete Briscoe. "A Few Powerful Words," *Daily Devotionals,* Dec 29, 2022.

[60]A.T. Robertson. *The Harmony of the Gospels* (New York: Harper & Row Publishers, 1950) 89-90.

[61]McKay, Michael. "Be Not Afraid." *Strive.* Kettering Health, summer 2022; 18-20.

[62]Brennan Manning. *The Rabbi's Heartbeat.* (Colorado Springs: NavPress, 2003).

[63]Spiro Zodiates ThD. *The complete Word Study Dictionary: New Testament.* (Chattanooga, TN: AMG Publishers, 1992), 687.

[64]Tim Chester. *The One True Gift.* (UK: The Good Book Company, 2017).

[65]Major W. Ian Thomas. *The Indwelling Life of Christ.* (Colorado Springs: Multnomah Books, 2006).

[66]Sally Lloyd-Jones. *The Jesus Storybook Bible.* (Grand Rapids, MI: Zonderkids, 2007).

[67]Anne Lamott, *bird by bird,* 100-101.

COLLABORATORS

author

Jan has been following hard after God for decades -- from her childhood home to a Catholic convent to her own home with a husband, children, and now grandchildren. All the time, Jan has seen God everywhere. And she's shared her experiences with God and His Word with her women's Bible study groups, in her devotional blog (www.abranchinthevine.com) and in her bible study book (*The With-ness of our God: Relationship in Every Dimension*).

In this latest project, *Glory in Disguise: Seeing God in our Every Day*, she teams up with her friend and fellow Christ-follower Penny Mandeville, to share experiences with God in everyday life situations -- from fun stories with grandkids to mundane stories of everyday life to serious stories of hard times. And all of these stories and scriptures reveal God's AHA's for her life and for yours too.

poet

Penny has been writing poetry for more than twenty years. Many of her poems have been for family birthdays or other celebrations. Often they are light hearted and silly as for a child's birthday. Others are personal and heartfelt like the ones remembering her parents who are now gone. She has been a Christian for 35 years and has enjoyed bringing her love of words, her love of God's Word, and her love of Jesus together.

cover designer

Jeremy is a freelance designer with a focus on brand identity and visual design for digital and print applications.

He has put his giftedness to work to his mom's writing projects -- Jan's devotional blog www.abranchinthevine.com, *The With-ness of our God* (2015), and now this project, *Glory in Disguise*. Thank you, my dear son!

You can view Jeremy's work at www.jloyd.net.

many thanks

- to my dear husband John, for your many hours of reading, proofing, and editing this manuscript. I couldn't have done it without you.

- to my friend and former teaching colleague, Barbara Sullivan, for reading and evaluating those early manuscript entries. Your love, encouragement, and critiques were invaluable.

- to our Branches prayer group. You have walked and prayed us through from those early days when this project was just a vision, and Penny and I just started writing.

- to my ZOOM Sisters prayer group. Your faithful prayer helped "walk this project home."

- to my dear grandsons Kaden Filson, Evan Loyd, Carter Loyd, Eli Filson, and William Filson; and to my darling granddaughter Claire Elizabeth Filson. Without you all, there would be fewer stories to tell.